HOW TO
BREAK OUT
OF PRISON

JOHN WAREHAM

HOW TO BREAK OUT OF PRISON
John Wareham

Welcome Rain New York

HOW TO BREAK OUT OF PRISON
Copyright © 2002 by John Wareham.
All rights reserved.

"Parental Love in the 21st Century"
Copyright © 2001 by John Suss, a.k.a. Jean Suss

Library of Congress CIP data available from the publisher.

Direct any inquiries to
Welcome Rain Publishers LLC

ISBN 1-56649-239-4

Printed in the United States of America by
HAMILTON PRINTING COMPANY

First Edition: July 2002
1 3 5 7 9 10 8 6 4 2

Dedicated to **Colonel Torquil MacLeod**, M.B.E.,

stalwart colleague, trusted friend, and lifetime inspiration

CONTENTS

How to Break *Into* Prison: A Pithy Prologue and Appreciation............... 11

PART ONE: **Who's Imprisoned and Why**

1. **Invisible Iron Balls** & Floating Magic Circles 19

2. **The Iron Ball Tagged <u>I</u>** & How Your Emotions Undermine You 33

3. **The Iron Ball Tagged <u>U</u>** & Why Your Stratagems Are Flawed 47

4. **The Iron Ball Tagged <u>O</u>** & Why Your Maneuvers Are Ineffective 61

5. **The Illusion that Locks the 3 Iron Balls in Place**
   & Why You Can't Escape.. 81

PART TWO: **Raise Cogitato**
& Begin to See the World With Open I's

6. **How to Wake Up in Prison**
   & Transmute Those Iron Balls into Magic Circles 99

7. **Magic Circle Number 1: The <u>I</u>ntegrated Value System**
   How It Transforms Mistakes into Virtues & Challenges
   into Savvy Choices.. 109

8. **How to Revise Your Alibi** & Overturn Your Conviction 131

9. **How to Create the Life of Your Dreams** A 7-Step Formula 151

10. **Cogitato's Message** In a Nutshell 161

PART THREE: **Enlist Advancio**
The Warrior Within Will Win the Day

11. **Magic Circle Number 2: The In-the Moment Grappling-Style**
   & How to Race a Motorcycle 165

12. **How to Talk Your Way Out of Trouble** & Into a Good Time 183

13. **Advancio's Message** In a Nutshell 189

PART FOUR: **Embrace Nurturio**
The Best Friend You Never Knew You Had

14. **Magic Circle Number 3: The Intact Sense of Self-Esteem**
   & How to Step Out of a Wheelchair............................. 193

15. **How to Preserve the Appearance of Integrity**
   When Push Comes to Shove.....................................209

16. **How to Create Some Love in Your Life**
   & Discover It in Unexpected Places.............................215

17. **Games Recidivists Play** & How To Pick Up and Go Home 225

18. **How to Overcome Temptation** Before It Overcomes You..............233

19. **Nurturio's Message** In a Nutshell............................239

20. **How to Complete a Journey** & Know Where You Are....................243

I have been studying how I may compare this prison where I live

unto the world.

—William Shakespeare, Richard II, Act V

How to Break *Into* Prison
A Pithy Prologue and Appreciation

hree days ago I was standing on the elevated ballroom stage of
London's five-star Dorchester Hotel, delivering an all-day, multi-
media, no-expenses-spared leadership seminar to a sellout audience of
chief executives, each of whom had paid $1,000 to share my insights.
The scent of roses suffused the air. Subtle lighting highlighted sump-
tuous wall coverings and refracted from the ivory-marble floor. A
hush descended as I stepped into a spotlight. And, of course, the
sound system was perfect.

Today, I'm contemplating an audience of twenty-five green-
uniformed inmates in a jam-packed twenty-by-fifteen-foot concrete
cell within the largest penal colony in the world, New York's Rikers
Island Jail. This particular assembly was selected from 200 applicants.
Most are due for release within the next six months. They want to be
in the class for several reasons: to ease the boredom, to show good
behavior, and, maybe, to learn something useful.

This is the first of thirteen weekly, three-hour Monday-morning
sessions. I have no lectern, no microphone, no slide show, and no
notes. Just chalk and a blackboard. The air is slightly stale, the fading
paint on the walls was once yellow. The bracing concrete floor is
sealed with gray rubber tiles. The delegates are sitting classroom-style
in stackable red plastic chairs polka-dotted with cigarette burns.
Those in the back have double-stacked their chairs for visibility,
thereby creating a mini-auditorium.

11

Fifteen are African-American. Eight are Hispanic. Two are Caucasian. There's an eclectic mix of tattoos, beards, sideburns, mustaches, and shaven heads. Three are wearing earrings. One is missing his front teeth. Many are doing time for drug-related crimes. Several have been committed for armed robbery. One, who attempted to stick up a hospital, got shot in the process and nearly bled to death; another seriously beat up his wife and her lover, and then turned himself in. Their ages range from twenty-something to forty-something. More than half have failed to graduate high school. Two are college dropouts. Most are very fit—one of the bonuses of incarceration is time to work out.

What, exactly, am I doing here? What am I going to say? Why should anyone listen?

To some extent, the answer to these questions lies in the vocation that brought me to this juncture.

Ever since I became self-employed at the tender age of twenty-four, my stock in trade has been people, and my job has been to judge them and help them. Like Macbeth's witches, I became an adviser, but to industrial kings—a modern soothsayer and seer, a psychologist and counselor: my task has been to foretell the future of would-be executives who are being considered for appointment to a seat in the corporate court.

Predicting an executive's future turns upon discovering repeating patterns of behavior. In this respect I am fortunate in being able to draw upon a rich source of information. Whenever my consulting firm appraises a person we work from 1) an in-depth interview; 2) a complete biography; 3) the candidate's actual past on-the-job performance; and 4) our own proprietary battery of psychological tests.

A lifetime in this industry enabled me to develop a conceptual framework that makes it possible to assess overall behavior from mere scraps of information. I was also fortunate in being trained for these tasks by one of the world's great industrial psychologists, Dr. Robert N. McMurry, who attended Sigmund Freud's psychoanalytic institute in Vienna, and was subsequently elected to the Chicago Psychoanalytic Society.

As a by-product of the advice I've been giving to chief executives, I also created a series of seminars on human behavior that I've presented to senior executives in just about every major world city. Some people call me a motivational speaker, but I shy away from that label. Sure, any good speaker is going to be uplifting. But my primary aim has always been to provide understanding resulting in action, not just enthusiasm. I try to leave a practical, pragmatic perspective that clarifies life's problems and makes them easier to resolve.

About five years ago a friend in the prison reform profession, Jennifer Wynn, author of the insightful and highly readable book, *Inside Rikers Island*, asked me to give a 90-minute class to a group of prison inmates. At the time, I wasn't sure that my material would be as helpful to inmates as it had been to executives, so I opted to run a class in public speaking. This proved successful and I was asked to run a series of classes. The original program had been founded to introduce Rikers' inmates to what one might call the four Cs—composition, cooking, computers, and conflict management. Given a free hand, I moved the focus of my teaching to subjects from my executive seminars, adding cognition, consciousness, and communication.

I called my class *How to Break Out of Prison* and created a manual with the same title. The suspicious guards who confiscated some of those handbooks were doubtless astonished to discover readings from, among others, Buddha, Confucius, Plato, Shakespeare, Sartre and Freud.

In fact, any such sage would have been delighted to confirm that the same faulty thinking can trap just about anyone. That's because *all prisons are mental prisons.* My own experience certainly confirms this to be true of inmates and executives alike. I also discovered that convicts could be less inclined than executives to deny the reality of their predicaments. And once they have a handle on their problems—along with some practical advice on how to deal with them—convicts are often more inclined to take remedial action. One way or another, then, my supposed "single session" morphed into a long-term seminar series.

The cynic, Ambrose Bierce, defined gratitude as "the hope that someone who has just done you a favor will do so again." When I contemplate that epigram I think of the loyal and illustrious corporate clientele that has entrusted leadership selection and development to my firm for better than quarter of a century. I am particularly indebted to the New York Department of Corrections, which brought more than safety, discipline, respect, and courtesy to a formerly notoriously out-of-control institution. They also created an enlightened environment.

I'm not sure how many other prison authorities would have tolerated my apparent sedition. Where else could I have coached inmates to debate such apparently heretical propositions as, "It is better to rob a bank than work for MacDonald's", or, "The destruction of the World Trade Center was justified?" To my surprise, the apparent profanity of such topics also miffed many inmates. It was that same contentiousness, however, that ultimately awakened them—first to the value of free and unfettered speech, then to the virtues of clear thinking, and, ultimately, to their own untapped potential.

I'm grateful beyond words to a loyal bevy of gifted courtroom attorneys, public speakers, and thinkers, including Bernie Mindich, John MacLean, Tovi Kratovil, Tom Morgan, Fiona Caulfield, Al Vogl, Shel Evans and Elise Kopczick. At the end of each semester, to showcase the newly acquired talents of my class, these friends and colleagues came out to Rikers to engage the cream of my class in formal parliamentary debate.

A vital debt is to the inmates who revealed their life stories, shared their insights, voluntarily completed my proprietary psychological questionnaires, and courageously took the floor to deliver some of the finest speeches I have ever heard. Some of their stories, altered to render identification impossible, of course, are included in this book. I'm especially grateful to the small band of apparently incorrigible recidivists whose unfortunate conditioning compelled them to try to disrupt some classes. In fact their neuroses merely played right into my own. "If you're looking for an argument," I would respond, banging my fist on the table, "then you've come to the right place, because I just *love* conflict!"

I'm obliged to the great poet John Suss for permission to include "Parental Love In The 21st Century."

Finally, of course, I'm delighted to thank John Weber, Charles Defanti, and Chuck Kim of Welcome Rain Publishers. I've had a lot of books published, but nobody has been more helpful, considerate or patient.

Without the help of the above people this book would not exist. Nor might my friends John Beaglehole and Allison Christians of Debevoise & Plimpton volunteered their time to help me to incorporate The Eagles Foundation, whose mission is to develop leadership potential among the incredibly talented ex-offenders who complete my classes. So if you're looking for a truly outstanding speaker—or cadre of same—to keynote a convention, enliven a discussion, or just make an audience feel that the world is a wonderful place, then go to www.wareham.org and email me. But read the book, first, of course.

PART ONE

WHO'S IMPRISONED AND WHY

Unreality is the true source of powerlessness.

What we do not understand we cannot control.

—Charles Reich

CHAPTER 1

Invisible Iron Balls
& Floating Magic Circles

It is only with the heart that one can see rightly;

what is essential is invisible to the eye.

—Antoine de Saint-Exupéry

José is in a rotten mood. He's sitting off to my right, somewhat on his own, one eye on the class and the other on me. My guess is that he wants us to notice the fire in his glare and the churlish flex in his thick, powerful forearms. He looks like a surly boxer—Mike Tyson, maybe—crouched on a stool between rounds. They tell me José's a problem in other classes, but he's not bothered me. Sure, he's a bit of a smart alec, and sure, he looks a little threatening, but I'm not worried. My hunch is that he's too concerned with his macho image to risk making himself seem foolish in front of his classmates by saying the wrong thing. Just the same, his narrowed eyes tend to suggest that he might just be biding his time.

"Unless our values, ideas, thoughts, and opinions accord with reality," I explain to the class, "then we're bound for trouble in the real world—"

José props himself forward in his chair and pounces. *"Reality!"* He spits the word, then pauses. "Tell me about this *real world*, teacher." He elaborately crosses his thick arms across his barrel chest. "Tell me what reality actually *is*."

The smart move is to defuse the query and then turn it back on him. "Hey, that's a good question, José—and, as I guess you know, it raises a series of profound issues. But you're a savvy guy—how might *you* describe reality?"

José's eyes flash. "Oh, no—*you're* the great expert," he says. "You're the one who *knows*. You're the *teacher* who's giving us the *big lecture*." The class falls silent. "You *say* you know, anyway. So *you* tell *me*—what is this reality that you're going on and on about?" He leans ostentatiously back in his chair, his smoldering eyes suddenly smug. He believes that just so long as he can be the arbiter of any answer, he's won. More than that, he wants the class to see that he can intimidate the instructor—and therefore them, too.

The class falls silent. They realize that José is spoiling for a fight. "Don't go there" is what their eyes are saying. Yet on another level, they need me to win the day. My mouth goes a little dry. Well, bone dry, actually. A line from Zorba the Greek floats like a butterfly into my mind: "Fools can ask questions that wise men cannot answer." No, let's not use *that* line. I turn to José and, drawing upon my full command of the English language, remain momentarily silent. What exactly do I need to achieve here? I see no choice but to accept his taunting enticement to join him in the ring—and I'll have to up the ante, that's for sure.

I take one step towards José and inject a shot of sarcasm into my voice. "What a *lucky* day it is for you, José. You could have asked just about anyone in the world that question, and my bet is that they'd have been struggling to come up with an answer to satisfy you."

"You're stalling." His thin mustache contemptuously curls. "What is reality? Tell me *now*?" He waves his hand over the class. "Tell us all. And tell us now."

"The reality of the matter, José"—I pause and cast a hopefully reassuring glance over the room—"is that you've asked the very question to which I alone in all the world might just happen to possess the *exact* answer you're seeking."

Realizing that I'm giving him back a little of his own medicine, José's eyes flash.

"Yes, that's right, José, I really can answer this for you, and for everyone else, too." I catch and hold his eye. "But *you* should be the judge of my answer, right, José?"

His nod is self-satisfied, but, sensing that I seem a little too confident, he's a touch tad less cocky.

"Well, that's good, because I know you're going to agree with it. And then you're going to want to commit it to memory. You might even want to engrave it on your heart. But, for the meantime, however, why don't you just pick up your pen and get ready to commit my answer to paper. I mean I don't want you forgetting it right away. And you have some paper there, don't you?"

He reaches for his yellow notepad. So, I have him under control. All I'll need now is a few good words. Let's hope I can come up with some. "So you get out your pen and I'll just grab this piece of chalk. Now, watch closely, José. I wouldn't want you to miss anything."

I turn to the blackboard and chalk up eight words, calling out each as it appears:

"When—the—student—is—ready,—the—teacher—appears."

I lay down the chalk and face the class. "What that means is that until a person is truly ready to listen, nobody can teach him anything. All sorts of people appear in our lives offering good advice on how we might overcome obstacles and enjoy success, but until we're ready to hear—to really listen and really hear—then we're effectively deaf. And as long as we remain deaf, reality delivers us some nasty blows—we might even wind up in prison. One day, however, things get so bad that a tiny voice inside of us tries to make itself heard. "I don't want to go on living like this," is what it says. With any luck at all, that faint voice registers in the brain and we begin to stir to the realization that we've been doing something wrong. Gradually, slowly, quietly, our ears and eyes become ready to open. Then one day, out of the blue, or so it seems to us, the very master teacher we most need to hear steps into our lives, and, even though our knee-jerk reaction is still resistance, we nonetheless find, for the first time in our lives, that we actually do hear some meaning in the words he offers."

I turn to José. He's not over his anger and he's not happy with the way the discussion has gone either. Just the same, I might just be getting through. I lock my eyes on his. "What I think such a teacher might want to say to you, José, is that we each create our own reality, and that yours, right now, is here within the walls of this prison. But you're not merely incarcerated in a cell—you're in a mental prison, too. That particular prison locks from the inside and the jailer is you. You locked yourself in and you hold the key, so only you can let yourself out. But right now, you'd rather fight than listen. I gather you behave like this way in every class, so I don't take it personally. I could say more, but for now, I'd rather finish this discussion of ours with a question than an answer. Do me a favor and come back next week to riddle me this: Why, really, do you continually wind up fighting with people in authority?" I pause. "And let me offer a hint to help you on your way: give some thought to your relationship with your father."

On the word *father*, José springs to his feet and waves a clenched fist in my face. "Don't you dare disrespect my fuckin' father," he shouts.

There's a guard up the corridor somewhere, but he'll be too late in arriving if José loses control. A couple of my burlier pupils move to restrain him. I shake my head, indicating to leave him alone. I step forward, wrap my arm around José's granite shoulders, and offer up what I hope will be a winning, empathetic smile. "I wouldn't dare criticize your father, José—I mean, you'd beat the shit out of me if I tried to pull that on you—right?"

"Yeah"—tears well in his eyes, as he drops his hands to his sides— "I'd beat the fuckin' shit out of you"—he smiles—"maybe."

LESSON #1
If you don't learn this you'll never get out of prison.

Why are you here?

That's the first question I ask of my inmate audience. And here come the answers.

> Because I did a foolish thing.
> Because I don't listen to people.
> Because I'm a victim of discrimination.
> Because God brought me here.

I listen carefully and go around the room. These answers always intrigue me. This is the first session, so everybody is being polite. Just the same, nobody seems to have a real handle on what went wrong in his life. So now it's my turn.

> But *why* did you do a foolish thing?

But *why* don't you listen to people?

But, *how*, exactly, did you come to be in a situation where some evil policeman was able to exercise his power over you?

But *why*—assuming for the moment that there is a God—did he reach the decision that you were incapable of looking after yourself?

This time the answers come back as blank stares. I grab a chalk and walk to the blackboard. Okay you guys, here it is, then, lesson number one:

> *You can't get out of prison until you know how you got in.*

All prisons are mental prisons, right? Of course they are. So, to show precisely how people from every walk of life unwittingly imprison themselves, I ask you, dear reader, to consider the story of a rich industrialist from the Northeast, who was horrified to find the Southern fisherman lying lazily beside his boat, smoking a pipe.

"Why aren't you out fishing?" asked the industrialist.

"Because I have caught enough fish for the day," replied the fisherman.

"Why don't you catch some more?"

"What would I do with them all?"

"You could make more money. With that you could have a motor fixed to your boat, and go and fish in deeper waters and catch more fish. Then you could buy nylon nets. These would bring you more fish and more money. Soon you would have enough money to own two boats. Then you'd be a rich man like me."

"What would I do then?"

"Then you could really enjoy life."

"What do you think I'm doing right now?"

A key point of the story is that *everyone*, from the richest to the poorest, must address the three basic challenges of life:

➤ To support oneself
➤ To express or fulfill oneself
➤ To create some love in one's life

The industrialist, already a rich man, finds his fulfillment in being a captain of industry. The fisherman earns enough to support himself, but apparently also derives enjoyment, fulfillment, and serenity from that role. He might also have a hobby or a spare-time interest. Love comes in many forms. Both the industrialist and the fisherman might already win affection from contacts made in their careers. Perhaps the industrialist's employees give him unstinting admiration and respect. Maybe the fisherman's customers like and admire and hold him in affection for bringing to market only the best of his catch. And, maybe, of course, both men are partners in happy love relationships. Anyway, here's the further point: we must surmount the challenges of life while maintaining a harmonious relationship with those around us.

If you saw the film *The Sixth Sense*, you'll likely remember the scene where the clairvoyant young boy, troubled by his ability to see another dimension, confides, "I see dead people." Well, I've been seeing something similar for some time, now.

➤ Rod served a year for drug dealing. He was a model prisoner, a handsome man with a first-class intellect and a knack for making friends. On the day of his release, I met Rod on Seventh Avenue, bought him a new set of clothes, and invited him to join us in a sailing expedition around the Statute of Liberty with a chief executive client of mine. It was a lot of fun. When we returned to land, however, Rod immediately disappeared. Then, when my client put on his coat and reached for the credit cards in his wallet, they were gone, too. Prison inmates serve time because they got caught and were convicted of breaking the law. They break the law because they cannot conceive of a way to win what they want from life without engaging in illegal activity. Rod's back in prison, by the way.

➤ Jack loves politics and everyone agrees that it's the field in which he should have made his career. Instead, he fell into corporate marketing and made a big success of it, until the day of his heart attack. The company put him out to pasture but very generously kept him on the payroll. These days, when he's not sitting on the porch dreaming of what might have been, he's out playing golf. Executives who stay with a corporation purely for the paycheck or the status or the power—when their hearts are telling them to quit—are corporate inmates. They stay, in essence, because they cannot imagine themselves capable of surmounting the challenges of life in any other milieu.

➤ Wayne got himself out of a tight financial situation by secretly charging personal expenses against the business operations funded by his partner. Initially the numbers were relatively small, and Wayne promised himself he'd make amends, some day. But that day never came, of course. The figures merely grew larger. First Wayne covered up by failing to produce an accounting. When that stratagem failed, he took to "cooking the books." The relationship soured, however, and the job became hell. Shysters who get what they want by means that are unethical—even if legal—do so because they can conceive of no honorable way of getting what they want. They might end up rich—they might even seem fulfilled—but in fact they are incarcerated by the knowledge that they never really won anything at all.

➤ Phil, a nationally ranked athlete earning $75,000 per performance, developed a drug habit, got into scrapes on and off the field, and beat his wife. By the time he appeared in my Rikers class, Phil was a shell of his former self—divorced, broke, and still in denial as to the source of his problems, which, by tortuous rationalizing, he ascribed not to himself but to God.

THE IMPRISONING TRIANGLE OF COMPROMISE

Let's be very clear. Rod, Jack, Wayne, and Phil—and anyone in a similar predicament—are making the same fundamental error. They're attempting to master the challenges of life by entering what I call the "imprisoning triangle of compromise." The three sides to that prison are:

1. **Need.** They desperately want something that they believe that they cannot get without compromising themselves. For many in my class this need is basic food and shelter. For corporate inmates it is security and status. At the far end of the spectrum it may be the so-called sweet life of glamour, celebrity, and unlimited largesse.

2. **Opportunity.** For many in my class, dealing drugs represents one opportunity to meet otherwise apparently unmeetable needs. Law-abiding corporate inmates perceive that opportunity in the apparent security of corporate pay and perquisites. For white-collar crooks—Enron executives and Arthur Andersen auditors spring to mind—the opportunity lies in corrupting the system. And, of course, for the crème de la crème of criminals the opportunity resides in outright embezzlement.

3. **Excuse.** Even a criminal likes to be able to rationalize his behavior. Rikers' inmates say that the only way to make ends meet is "to pick up a gun and do what a man has to do" in order to put some bread on the table. Corporate inmates say that they're hanging on in order to pay the mortgage on the lovely house in the suburbs and to put their kids through the finest schools and colleges. The likes of Enron executives and auditors will protest that they were *really* trying to protect the investing public.

By my reckoning, imprisoned people comprise addicts of all stripes, including workaholics, incorrigible spendthrifts, and mindless status seekers, all of whom are merely attempting to anaesthetize the distress that springs from not fulfilling their true needs and missions. The drug of choice becomes the triangle of compromise. It represents an irresistible opportunity to intoxicate the underlying need, and create a first-rate excuse.

Paradoxically, dealing with "real" convicts has caused me to recognize an increasing number of inmates unconfined by concrete and steel. Most look and sound like losers, but from a distance many can seem like winners, too. The trouble is that those who resort to cheating lose, even when they seem to win.

I'm often asked to contrast and compare my two audiences. Well, bear in mind that corporate executives and crime czars have a lot in common. Successful drug dealers, for example, possess many vital corporate skills. They negotiate with suppliers, develop marketing strategies and budgets, recruit and motivate salespeople, and keep a sharp eye on the bottom line—all under incredibly intense pressure. Just about any truly competent upper-level drug operator could lead a legitimate business unit. Beyond that, however:

- Executives are better educated and more sophisticated in terms of business. They appreciate my specialist perspective and are keen to get a handle on the hard-won lessons I've gleaned in my discipline. They're also more tunnel-visioned, somewhat blasé in the presence of a great idea, and, with notable exceptions, less inclined to give up the prejudices they've assembled over the years.

- Prison audiences are usually more conscious of their predicaments, and once I get past their outer shells, somewhat less inclined to cling to pretense or denial, keener to face up to their situations and set about changing them, often much more open to new ideas, and especially quick to seize upon and apply practical suggestions.

In fact, some of my inmate students are sometimes a little *too* keen to apply my insights. They've taught me to think long and hard before dispensing advice. However, I don't want them to apply nuggets of information in a vacuum. I want them to proceed from a deeper understanding their own underlying conditioning.

One way to achieve this is to have them complete a questionnaire and subsequently use it to help them analyze their lives. I'd like to offer you the same opportunity, *and I'd like you to do it right now.* This way your answers won't be influenced by the concepts I'll be laying out on the pages that follow. So, get yourself a pencil, and complete my Condensed Life Insight Questionnaire—the Wareham CLIQ—a battery of incomplete sentences. Complete each sentence stem as truthfully and spontaneously as you can, bearing in mind that your first answer is likely to be just about as good as anything else.

The Wareham Condensed Life Insight Questionnaire (CLIQ)

1. I am very _____
2. My greatest talent _____
3. People think that I _____
4. My parents always told me I should _____
5. My father _____
6. If only my father _____
7. Obeying my father _____

8. My mother _____

9. If only my mother _____

10. As a child I loved to _____

11. I was expected to become _____

12. The best measure of personal success is _____

13. The defining moment of my life _____

14. I become anxious when_____

15. The person who most influenced the development of my
    personality was _____
    who taught me _____

16. If I can't get what I want, I_____

17. The main driving force in my life is _____

18. What I need most in a partner is_____

19. I am trying to overcome _____

20. I feel guilty when I _____

21. Realistically, to enjoy a satisfactory lifestyle I need an annual
    income of approximately $_____

22. My way of winning the struggle to get what I want is to _____
    _____

23. I persuaded him to change his mind by _____

24. I feel I am being held back by _____

25. I get irritated when they_____

26. The thing I like about myself is_____

27. What gets me into trouble is _____

28. When a peer does better, I_____

29. If I would only_____

30. I was happiest_____

31. Compared with others, I_____

32. I fall into a blue mood when _____

33. I suffered most from _____

34. My most significant achievement _____

35. My greatest fear_____

36. If I could have any career I desired,
    I'd be a _____
    because _____

37. I lose my temper if _____

38. I wish _____

39. My dream _____

40. On a scale from a worst of 1 to a best of 10, I rate my current situation as:

Job _____

Finances _____

Personal fulfillment _____

Love relationship _____

Now that you've completed the CLIQ—which you really *must* do to get all the benefits this book has to offer—let's get back to the classroom and take Wareham's one-minute semester in human psychology. I turn to the board and write:

I am what I EAT!

E stands for Emotions, A stands for Actions, and T stands for Thoughts—okay?

I draw three circles and write in the words to drive home the point.

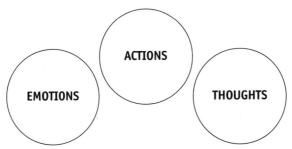

There's a problem with this diagram. It fails to reflect the fact that our emotions, actions, and thoughts don't operate independently of each other. In fact, they overlap. So the diagram should look like this:

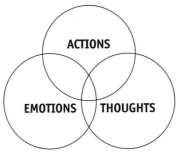

The Three Invisible Iron Balls

You're in jail because your three circles aren't working properly. Think of them as iron balls that are weighing you down and holding you back. If you stop struggling for just a minute to study them, you'd see that each bears a brass tag. One is tagged <u>I</u>. One is tagged <u>O</u>. And one is tagged <u>U</u>. So, together these three tags very appropriately spell out IOU.

The I stands for Injured Sense of Self-Esteem, the O stands for Obsolete Grappling Style, and the U stands for Unrealistic Value System. These three invisible iron balls are messing up your life and leaving you feeling queasy and conflicted. That queasiness springs from a very specific dilemma. Your mouth tells everyone that you're fully in charge of your life, but there's a sickness in your heart and behavior that spells out an altogether different story. You're trapped in the *illusion of autonomy*: you *think* you know what you're doing—but in reality you don't! So, ultimately we can reduce the whole problem to a very simple acronym—*My IOU is making me Ill*—and diagram the conundrum something like this:

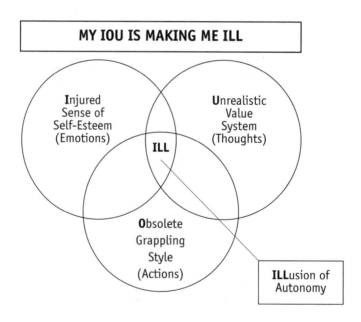

The whole thing reminds me of the three balls hanging above a pawnshop that represent—so the saying goes—the two-to-one odds against ever redeeming the item in hock. In this case, of course, the redeemable item is your own life.

The catch is that most people don't realize their lives are in hock to anything, and argue the point if you try to tell them otherwise. But I'm getting ahead of myself. Let's take a closer look at each of these iron balls and you'll see what I'm saying.

CHAPTER 2

The Iron Ball Tagged I

& How Your Emotions Undermine You

Every man treats himself

as society treats the criminal.

—Harvey Ferguson

"The notion that *any* senior member of this organization might suffer feelings of inferiority is utterly *preposterous*!" exclaims Baxter Barrow.

I'm running an in-house seminar in the boardroom of a British conglomerate, and Baxter is a priggish, pudding-faced, fiftyish engineer touted to be the heir apparent to the chief. I'm not surprised that the notion of an inferiority complex has him vexed. His haughtiness and irritation suggest a man imprisoned by the very sense of inferiority that he's so desperate to deny. He's doubtless frightened of revealing his insecurities in front of the other executives, especially since he'd like to believe that they're his inferiors. So, like our old friend José back in Rikers, Baxter's trying to shore up his big-shot status by belittling the outside expert.

"You may well be right, Baxter," I reply with a grin. "Perhaps there's something in the sweet English air that immunizes its executives from feelings of inferiority." I look over the twenty or so faces. "Does anyone else feel like sharing a point of view?"

Baxter's putative peers don't seem keen to jump into the silence. Suddenly, the chief executive leans forward in his chair. "I read that handout on the inferiority complex, John," he says in his no-nonsense North of England accent, "and I have to confess that it irked me, too"— he shakes his head, sadly—"but for a different reason." He pauses and cracks a big smile. "I got upset because the article perfectly described the faults and foibles that I was hoping to keep hidden from everybody." The smiles and chuckles gradually become good-natured laughter. Baxter is chagrined and perplexed, of course. He simply can't figure out why his chief would admit to any such emotional shortcoming.

The Solser Syndrome

The notion of *feelings of inferiority* was first promulgated nearly a century ago by pioneering psychologist Alfred Adler, who noted that such feelings "manifest in the presence of a problem for which an individual is improperly adapted or equipped, and highlight his conviction that he is unable to deal with it."

Such a person, according to Adler, suffered an "inferiority complex." Just about everybody who heard the expression knew somebody who suffered from precisely such a problem—though seldom, of course, their own wonderful selves—and this memorable coinage went straight into the collective unconscious.

Then, more recently, psychologist Dr. Nathaniel Branden put a positive spin on the idea by coming up with the rather less threatening, more politically correct term, *self-esteem*. If you don't possess self-esteem—or enough of it—then according to Branden, you're a Sufferer of Low Self-Esteem, or in my coinage, a SOLSER.

So far so good—but how, exactly, does one define self-esteem? This is a great question deserving of a jargon-free answer. Okay, then, stripped to its essentials, self-esteem may be defined by two key parts:

> ➤ Confidence in one's ability to address life's basic challenges. The feeling that, yes, I can survive in this world; I am capable of handling whatever life throws at me; I can surmount obstacles and wrest what I need and want from life.

The second element is no less important:

> ➤ The feeling that one truly deserves whatever good fortune one earns, and is therefore entitled to hold onto it.

By definition then, Solsers are less than confident of their ability to address the challenges of life. And, if they happen to fall upon good times, they typically feel undeserving and find a way to undermine their own successes—a syndrome we'll look at more closely later.

In reality, most people suffer from low self-esteem. In a lifetime of evaluating outwardly confident executives, I've come to realize that low self-esteem is pervasive and only a minority of executives are truly confident. This is not to say that a shaky sense of self-esteem need impede a person's career. Indeed, it often works the opposite way, as we'll soon see under the heading "How Solsers Cope."

Feelings of inadequacy tend to be universal for good reason: human beings really are among the physically weakest creatures on earth; children remain dependent upon the nurturing of parents for longer than any other species; and now technological advancement demands that even more time be dedicated to higher education, delaying entry into the "real world."

TOXIC PARENTING AND THE POISON IVY SYNDROME

The other key problem, of course, is *toxic parenting*. This comes in more forms than most people realize. Physical abuse and neglect head, but do not end, the list of toxicities. Let's take a quick look at a couple of common patterns.

What I call the Poison Ivy Syndrome is relatively common in many so-called privileged homes. Here the child is cosseted and insulated from the world and pampered and indulged, given the finest possible education, often along with a trust fund. Unfortunately, that child gains minimal experience in cooperating, contributing, and sharing with others, becoming an emotional cripple instead of learning to stand on his or her own feet. In so-called adulthood, such a person can seem poised and brilliant to the point of arrogance. Pervasive feelings of inferiority—along with resentment and anger—lie behind that cocky mask, however, because the sufferer knows, albeit unconsciously, that he or she is not truly qualified to deal with the everyday challenges of life. I have evaluated countless M.B.A. graduates in their late twenties and early thirties whose grades were outstanding but whose perspective on life was decidedly immature, whose emotional intelligence was close to nil, and in whom feelings of inferiority were rife. Consider, for example, the case of the reclining executive candidate:

A thirty-nine-year-old, six-foot-three-inch candidate to lead a major division within a Fortune 500 company presented himself for his interview with me in an immaculate, tailored suit. As he seated himself upon my leather couch, I noted that, despite his M.B.A. and Ph.d. from fine Ivy League universities, he was earning somewhat less than I would have expected, so I invited him to comment. He suddenly rose to his feet. "Would it be okay if I remove my shoes?" he asked. Though I'd never had such a request before, I could see no harm. But then he not only removed his shoes, but also tucked a pillow under his head and spread himself out on the sofa. As the interview progressed, he gradually folded into the fetal position. The only thing missing was the thumb in the mouth.

A related syndrome is that of the *mixed-message home*. In this case, to most observers, including the children, the home environment seems to be almost ideal. The child is well cared for and sent to good schools—yet still somehow becomes something of an anxious underachiever. The hard-to-spot problem is that the child is embraced on one level, yet rejected on another. One way or another, one or both parents don't really want the kid around. This situation burdens the child with a ton of free-floating anxiety.

The parents may also subtly impart self-esteem-sabotaging dictums, ranging from, "You're just not good enough," to "You'll screw up your life." Such dictums typically drop, of course, from the lips of hyper-competitive parents who are fearful—usually as a result of their own rotten parenting—that their children may outperform them.

THE OUTSIDER SYNDROME

Does my reclining and fetally curled candidate's feelings of inferiority—along with the unusual coping device he's honed—differ very much from those of my class of prison inmates? Well, they're incarcerated within an actual jail, of course, whereas he's not. The key difference, however, lies in the fact that social conditioning has a lot to do with their feelings of inferiority.

Forget for a moment about skin color and think about this: most of my inmate students are the descendants of slaves. According to the infamous Dred Scott decision of the U.S. Supreme Court, slaves were ruled to be less than human, and thus were not entitled to equality under the Constitution. They were deliberately left uneducated and schooled only in obedience and conformity. Those who rebelled against the system were either whipped into submission or killed. *Feelings of inferiority were systematically instilled.*

A similar kind of thing happened in Rome, of course—but with a couple of crucial differences. First, a Roman slave could earn his freedom. And, second, if he did, he was physically indistinguishable from his fellow citizens.

In the United States, however, for two hundred years, virtually all the citizens were white and all the slaves black. And, of course, when Abraham Lincoln finally got around to freeing the slaves *they remained black.* Their color continued to mark them as supposedly inferior people. They were still relatively uneducated, they had no resources, they still thought like slaves, their feelings of inferiority were not dispelled—quite the opposite—and, of course, the law continued to enshrine social apartheid. As the writer James Baldwin observed in *Notes of a Native Son,* "All over Harlem, Negro boys and girls are growing into stunted maturity, trying desperately to find a place to stand: and the wonder is not that so many are ruined, but that so many survive."

This whole syndrome is neatly displayed in an ironic piece of African-American humor:

> A black brother died and found himself at the gates of Heaven.
>
> "Record your name in this book," said Saint Peter.
>
> As the brother did so, Saint Peter looked around. "Where's your horse?" he asked.
>
> "I ain't riding," said the man.
>
> "Well, that's too bad, because we're not taking walkers this week. To enter here you have to be riding."
>
> Dejectedly, the brother walked on down the road toward the bus station for those going the Other Way. He had almost arrived when he came upon a white man. "Where you going?" asked the brother.
>
> "To Heaven," replied Whitey.
>
> The brother shook his head. "You ain't gonna get in," he said. "I just came from the pearly gates and Saint Peter ain't taking walkers—only riders."

They sat on a rock to contemplate their predicament. Suddenly, the brother had an idea. "Hey! I know how we can both get in," he said excitedly. "You jump up on my back and *I'll* be the horse."

Whitey beamed approvingly, mounted the black man's shoulders, and they sallied to the celestial entrance. With the brother breathing heavily beneath him, Whitey leaned forward and rapped on the pearly gates.

"Who's that?" called Saint Peter.

"It's me, a good and honest man," called Whitey.

"Are you walking?" asked Saint Peter.

"No, I'm riding."

"All right then, *you* can come on in," said Saint Peter, "but you'll have to leave your *horse* outside."

One might feel that the problems of slavery and exclusion have disappeared into history and folklore, and no longer apply. Consider, then, Michael's brief speech to my class on "the defining moment of my life."

The defining moment of my life came when my mother moved our family from Harlem to Atlanta. I was eight years old at the time. When I got to Atlanta a group of kids offered to teach me how to buy a hamburger. I said I already knew how to do that, but they just laughed and led me to the local diner. My first mistake, of course, was to try to walk in the front door. That was reserved for whites only. They were sitting at tables and eating their lunches. When I got kicked out my friends just laughed and led me to a side door reserved for colored folks. I watched as each in turn climbed up onto a box in front of a window to place their orders. Then they took their hamburgers across the street, crouched down with their hands on their knees, and peered back with a clear line of sight through the door and into the window. I had no idea of what they were doing. I simply ordered my hamburger, then joined them across the street to eat it. "Why were you crouching like that?" I asked. "What were you staring at?" They just laughed again. "We're looking out for you," they replied. "From back here we can see into the kitchen.

We wanted to make sure that the white folks in that hamburger joint hadn't been urinating on your hamburger."

Michael, a sensitive, handsome man in his forties, related that story in a year 2000 class. Michael has very strong writing skills, by the way. He's realistic, too. When we last spoke, his goal was to continue to write while supporting himself sweeping the streets in New York's Ready, Willing, and Able program. I praised his choice, and, hoping it might inspire, gave him a copy of George Orwell's *Down and Out in Paris and London.* I know that Michael's talents fit him for higher callings. I could also see that in the short term, anyway, his self-esteem was so low that a higher goal might just set him up for failure.*

Michael's story is typical of what I hear in my class. Just about every last one of my students is from a broken, fatherless home, is poorly educated, possesses minimal skills, and precious little hope of ever finding employment. Just about every last student has been the victim of a systemic assault on his self-esteem.

The effect of such a battering was well illustrated in a series of recent experiments conducted by Clark Steele, a psychologist leading a team of researchers at Stanford University, looking at how certain groups perform under pressure.**

> Steele and Joshua Aronson found that when they gave a group of Stanford undergraduates a standardized test and told them that it was a measure of their intellectual ability, the white students did much better than their black counterparts. But when the same test was presented simply as an abstract laboratory tool, with no relevance to ability, the scores of blacks and whites were virtually identical. Steele and Aronson attribute this disparity to what they call "stereotype threat": when black students are put into a situation where they are confronted

---

*I happened to relate this story to a society matron and couldn't help smiling at her response. "It's good for him to sweep the streets," she said, "there's real dignity in that kind of work." She's right, of course. My bemusement came from the fact that she lives in three homes: a commodious Hamptons retreat, a spectacular Arizona villa—and, paradoxically, a rent-controlled Manhattan apartment. The moral, of course, is that the legacy of slavery lives on.
**Reported in *The New Yorker*, August 21 & 28, 2000.

with a stereotype about their group—in this case one having to do with intelligence—the resulting pressure causes their performance to suffer.

What is perhaps even more interesting is that Steele and others have found the same stereotype threat at work in any situation where groups are depicted in negative ways.

Give a group of qualified women a math test and tell them it will measure their quantitative ability and they will do much worse than equally skilled men will; present the same test simply as a research tool and they'll do just as well as the men.

Or consider a handful of experiments conducted by one of Steele's former graduate students, Julio Garcia, a professor at Tufts University:

Garcia gathered together a group of white athletic students and had a white instructor lead them through a series of physical tests: to jump as high as they could, to do a standing broad jump, and to see how many push-ups they could do in twenty seconds. The instructor then asked them to do the tests a second time, and, as you'd expect Garcia found that the students did a little better on the tasks second time around. Then Garcia ran a second set of students through the tests, this time replacing the instructor between the first and second trials with an African-American. Now the white students ceased to improve on their vertical leaps. He did the experiment again only this time he replaced the white instructor with a black instructor. In this trial the white students actually jumped less high than they had the first time around. Their performance on the push-ups, though, was unchanged in each of the conditions. There is no stereotype, after all, that suggests that whites can't do as many push-ups as blacks. The task that was affected was the vertical leap, because of what our culture says: white men can't jump.

In his autobiography, Malcolm X observes that such stereotyping became "the first major turning point in my life." It came in a private discussion with his English teacher and career counselor, a white man whom Malcolm admired. When Malcolm expressed his ambition to become a lawyer, the counselor leaned back in his chair and clasped his hands behind his head. "Malcolm, one of life's first needs is to be realistic. Don't misunderstand me, now. We all like you, you know that. But you've got to be realistic about being a nigger. A lawyer—that's no realistic goal for a nigger. You need to think about something you *can* be." Malcolm believed that the advice was well intentioned. He observed, however, that he alone was advised against the career of his choosing, even though he was a top student. "It was then that I began to change," he notes. He gave up on his studies, became "delinquent," and soon enough fell into a life of crime.

The root of his resentment did not so much lie in the careless use of an ugly slur. It stemmed, rather, from the belief held against him that, despite how smart he had proved himself to be, "apparently I was still not intelligent enough, in their eyes, to become whatever *I* wanted to be."

One could say that Malcolm should have fought against that prejudice then and there—as he later did. In my own experience with many intelligent young African-Americans, I have observed that upon weighing all the obstacles that lie before them, it is all too often *realistic* to feel overwhelmed by life's basic challenge—that of supporting oneself—and to see only three ways to ease one's problems: dishing hamburgers, selling drugs, or using them.

HOW SOLSERS COPE

The overriding goal of the sufferers of low self-esteem—Solsers—is to gain superiority over their perceived inadequacies. Adler created a controversy by observing that Solsers typically gravitate to careers and lifestyles that deftly and exactly mask the underlying shortcomings. Thus, behind the facade, the clown is often suicidal, the clergy materialistic, the police harboring criminal tendencies, and many a highly publicized dynamic, audacious executive is in fact a frightened fellow who needs what Marla Maples—who I'm sure draws upon tremendous expertise as exwife of tycoon, presidential candidate, and Miss America connoisseur, Donald Trump—called the "drug of attention" to anaesthetize his feelings of inferiority.*

---

*Hearing this theory a waggish pupil apparently enquired of Herr Adler, "Does this mean, professor, that psychologists are crazy?" The answer, of course, is many are: psychiatrists are reported to have the highest suicide rate of any profession.

In fact, Solsers generally split into two groups: those who address their problems and those who focus on their feelings. Examples of people who have addressed their problems and transformed a potentially crippling weakness into a formidable strength are legion. Countless Olympic athletes have been spurred by the need to overcome the perceived ignominy of a physical weakness. The Roman orator Demosthenes trained himself to overcome a stutter by filling his mouth with pebbles and shouting into the wind; British Prime Minister Winston Churchill and actors James Earl Jones and Bruce Willis did much the same. And, of course, outstanding executives typically spring from immigrant homes whose children are mightily propelled to overcome a perceived ethnic stigma. All these people seek both to get rid of and to deny their feelings of inferiority by becoming superachievers—which entails, of course, working long and hard to alter their situations and circumstances. My own observation is that the achievement seldom suffices to quench the underlying demons, but in the grand scheme of things, who would quibble?

THE SOLSER'S MISTAKE

The second group of people is more interesting—and more depressing. They make a mistake. Instead of working to improve their situations, they merely attempt to make themselves feel better. They perceive an overwhelming world and make the judgment—usually unconsciously—that they don't possess the wherewithal to succeed in life. If they do manage to fall upon good times, they feel unworthy and find ways to sabotage themselves. These people typically labor under the heavy weight of a rotten upbringing. Such individuals are routinely encountered in corporate life. They're the empty suits, tap dancers, boy scouts, bureaucrats, and autocrats—the assorted incompetents who seem okay but never actually achieve anything. They use all sorts of coping devices to make themselves feel better. They attend meetings and demonstrate a command of concepts and jargon. They dedicate great chunks of time to getting organized. They hone their titles, resumes, and alibis—their finger-pointing and blame-shifting skills are almost inspiring. They can do everything except make and execute a commonsense decision. It is a small step, once in this pool, to outright dishonesty, to claiming nonexistent results, credentials, or even expenses.

What differentiates the moderately insecure person from this level of Solser is the ability to cooperate, contribute, and share with others. "The only individuals who can really meet and master the problems of life," says Adler, "are those who show in their striving a tendency to enrich everyone else, those who forge ahead in such a way that others benefit too." In fact, at the deepest level of their psyches, seriously impaired Solsers find it impossible to believe that they can actually render a valuable contribution. They may possess the intelligence and technical skill to contribute, but their capacity to act is hopelessly undermined by feelings of inferiority.

It is tempting to believe that education can resolve their problems. Unless one addresses self-esteem issues, however, the trouble persists. Before becoming a violent criminal, Joel, for example, completed an Ivy League degree in literature and politics with outstanding grades. The world was open to him, but he fell into a life of crime. After serving his time, he once again failed to seek challenging employment and a good salary. Instead, he settled into a totally unfulfilling janitorial role. When urged to seek something more fitting of his considerable talents he'd tell you that "the white establishment" was holding him back. The real problem was that behind the angry mask, he was too fearful to trust his own abilities. Even though he was outwardly a free man he remained imprisoned by his lack of self-esteem. The hidden benefit was that he didn't risk failure. On the bright side, when apprised of his own unconscious motivations, Joel quit his self-defeating ways and went on to win dramatic career advancement.

So, now, we're back in prison, and my two-hour session is coming to a close. Some in the audience have heard me very clearly. Others aren't so sure. I address both groups.

"So, I bet you see yourself as victims. And the truth of the matter, as I hope I've made clear, is that you are. You've been mindlessly mistreated by society, and your parents, too, probably. The consequence is—and some of you are going to deny this—that your self-esteem has taken a terrible beating, and your thinking has been messed up. Don't get me wrong. One of the most important things I've learned in running seminars for both executives and inmates is that if you've somehow managed to land in this Rikers program, then you're probably as intelligent as anyone I know or will ever meet. But some of you won't be ready to believe that right now, either. Well, William Shakespeare—who might not have been the utterly good guy that many people like to believe—has a message that might just set you in a frame of mind to see that even the smartest people can turn prison time into an ultimately enlightening experience. Let's look at his sonnet, number 119."

> *What potions have I drunk of siren tears*

A "potion" might be a drug, "siren tears" would be tears that come after we give in to temptation.

> *Distilled from limbecks foul as hell within*

A "limbeck" is a contraption for distilling alcohol. He's saying that evil in his heart created the unhappy potions that he drank.

> *Applying fears to hopes and hopes to fears*

His state of mind alternated between bravado and anxiety.

> *Still losing, when I saw myself to win.*

Nothing worked. He imagined he might win, but he finished up a loser.

> *What wretched errors hath my heart committed*
> *When it hath thought itself so blessed never*

His wildly foolish heart lead him astray.

> *How have mine eyes out of their spheres been fitted*
> *In the distraction of this madding fever.*

He was effectively blinded by his passion. All bad news so far, but there's good news coming.

> *Oh benefit of ill now I find true*
> *That better is by evil still made better*
> *And ruined love, when it is built anew*
> *Grows fairer than at first, more strong, far greater.*

"So, what did he realize—who wants to jump in here—?"

"He's saying, sir"—the voice belongs to Dwayne, who, save for the tapestry of scars on his face, looks like an NBA basketball star—"that he was all fucked up, and he fucked up other people's lives, too, but

now that he's got a handle on his problems, his rotten behavior is helping him to love those people even more."

"Hey, that's great. Now read me the last two lines. And call me
John, by the way."

Thus I return rebuked to my content,
And gain by ills thrice more than I have spent.

"So, how's his self-esteem, Dwayne?"
"He's feeling better about himself."
"How much better?"
"Three times better."

CHAPTER 3

The Iron Ball Tagged <u>U</u>

& Why Your Stratagems Are Flawed

The easiest thing of all is to deceive oneself;
for what a man wishes, he generally believes to be true.

—Demosthenes

"It is heretical to argue that God does not exist!"

Berry's eyes are bulging and the vein on his neck looks as if it might just pop. He's a natural public speaker with a dramatic flair, but he's about to mess up his big chance to win selection to the three-man Rikers debating team.

He doesn't realize that I assigned him the task of leading a team to affirm a set of arguments that run counter to his Christian values and beliefs precisely because his analytical powers need honing. Unfortunately, in the face of this challenge, Berry's mood has turned to two-parts passion and three-parts rage.

"I simply will not stand before this class and make that argument—not for you, not for anybody. No way, man, no way!"

All eyes turn to me. How will I deal with Berry's principled stance?

"There's a God, right, Berry?"

"You bet there is."

"Would he like you to outwit the devil?"

"Yes."

"But what if the devil used mind-boggling arguments to prove that there really is no God?"

"I'd demolish him."

"But first you'd have to hear his arguments, right?"

"Maybe."

"And that's what we're trying to discover right now. That's why I've set you the challenge of playing—*playing*, mind you—devil's advocate."

This discussion is merely aggravating Berry.

"Okay, then, Berry—let's forget the debate for a moment." I draw a line down the middle of the blackboard. At the top of one column I write, "God does not exist." At the top of the other column I write, "God exists." I look over the class. "What arguments might the devil make to prove that God doesn't exist?"

Hutch steps into the silence. "The suffering of children," he says. "Some people say that if there really was a God, that wouldn't happen."

"Right. That's a great argument. Now, how might God reply, Berry?"

Berry springs to his feet. "This is sacrilege, man. I can't sit here and listen to this shit." He springs to his feet, struts to the door, and roils out into the corridor. All eyes turn to me.

I search the faces in the class. "Would anybody else like to suggest God's reply to the question of the suffering of children?"

There's a long silence, but finally Dwayne steps in. "God has given man free will."

"How does that work?"

"Well, God's teaching *us* to be responsible for looking out for our children. We have to address that problem for ourselves."

"Yeah . . ." A soft voice sounds behind me. It belongs to Berry. He steps back into the room and offers a sheepish grin. "So the problem is with man, not God."

"Good thinking, Berry. But let's save the debate till next week. Right now I want to discuss the question of why we human beings are so often irrational."

"We're gonna talk about stinking thinking?"

"Yes, Hutch—where do you think it comes from?"

"Search me."

"Drugs, maybe."

"It comes from an unrealistic value system."

"What does that mean, really?"

"It means believing things that aren't true or don't make sense."

"Why do people do that?"

"Now, *that*, is a big question, Hutch."

Why, really, do apparently rational human beings insist on being "right" when it would be a whole lot smarter to be "wrong?" Why do we get so angry when other people's ideas fail to accord with our own? Why do we mock and block new concepts and beliefs? Why do we run away—literally—from an idea we don't like?

The answer lies in the fact that the human mind displays some all-too-human idiosyncrasies—and that until we understand them, we can be imprisoned by our own thinking processes.

THE UNREALISTIC VALUE SYSTEM
& How It Imprisons Even the Sanest People

These days most people realize that the basic difference between people comes down to the beliefs they hold and the values they assign to their ideas. They often appreciate, too, that values are the prime determinants of *behavior*, including, choice of dress, job, friends, home, entertainment, God—and much, much more. What very few people realize, however, is that even the sanest among us routinely become imprisoned in unrealistic value systems, yet because of the way the mind works, mistakenly believe they're in some kind of heaven—and fight for the right to remain incarcerated. Let's look at ten concepts, and you'll see what I mean.

1. BELIEFS ARE NOT FACTS.

A belief is not a fact, so the value we assign to a belief is merely that of an opinion. Therefore, no one can *prove* his beliefs superior to anyone else's. No one can prove, for example, that belief in God, free speech, abortion, communism, financial success—or whatever—is good or bad, right or wrong.

Osama bin Laden could no more prove that infidels are more worthy to die than the "Reverend" Jerry Falwell can prove his notion that God would rather talk to a Christian than a Jew (or that one Teletubbie is worthier than another, for that matter).

2. WE SELDOM KNOW WHY WE THINK WHAT WE DO.

It would be nice if some all-seeing or visionary educator were to show us exactly how the world works. Armed with that insight, we could surely go on to enjoy problem-free lives. Instead, however, we acquire our most basic beliefs by a process akin to osmosis. First, our parents tell us what to believe about the world and instill the values of the culture which we absorb in order to survive with a minimum of pain. Teachers, professors, priests, and politicians subsequently continue this process of indoctrination, pontificating to us from positions of authority. Ultimately, these notions, imprinted into our brain cells, become the prism through which we perceive "reality." In fact, we *remain* unaware of exactly what we believe or why, even as we reflexively access our unconscious beliefs to support supposedly conscious decision-making processes.

3. WE MISTAKENLY PUT OUR FAITH IN "HIGHER HEADS."

That we absorb our values from parents, teachers, professors, priests—people we *look up to* in the most literal sense—usually serves to impair our thinking processes even further.

We become conditioned—physically, emotionally, and intellectually—to looking up to authority, accepting the values of authority figures, and mindlessly relying upon their dictums.

The end result is that we come to distrust our own judgment and instinctively seek guidance from *a head that is higher than our own.*

The head itself may belong to some form of parental surrogate such as a boss or a mentor. Or, the head may belong to a divine emissary such as a rabbi, priest, shaman, or, increasingly, a soothsayer via the phone or Internet.

Savvy leaders, appreciating the process, commonly attempt to exploit it. Thus, the monarch sits on his throne, the priest climbs up into his pulpit, the office of the chief executive commands the highest floor, and the faces of political dictators and assorted Big Brothers peer down from massive billboards.

Even in the supposedly egalitarian United States, the giant sculptured heads of former United States presidents gaze down from Mount Rushmore.

George Bernard Shaw noted the syndrome, observing, "We are overrun with Popes. From curates and governesses, who may claim a sort of professional standing, to parents and uncles and nursery maids and school teachers and wiseacres generally, there are scores of thousands of human insects groping through our darkness by the feeble phosphorescence of their own tails, yet ready at a moment's notice to reveal the will of God on every possible subject."

Unfortunately, these Higher Heads have the capacity to control our emotions as well as our thoughts. We commonly pay a price in guilty feelings when we rebel—or even *think* about rebelling—against the pervasive injunctions of the Higher Head. Our programming is akin to that of the newborn elephant chained to a heavy stake so that it cannot stray beyond the circle circumscribed by the tether. When fully grown, the most powerful beast on earth can now be fully restrained by twine tied to a stick. It doesn't stray because it has been conditioned to believe that it cannot—and fears punishment if it tries. We can all too easily become similarly enslaved by the various Higher Heads that effectively imprison us within circles that soon enough become inescapable ruts.

4. OUR VALUES ARE RARELY CONSISTENT.

Since our values are unconsciously acquired from disparate sources, it is normal for *conflicting* value constellations to find a happy haven inside our skulls—without our realizing it.

The Africans have a saying: "In the beginning we had the land and the White Man had the Bible. Then we had the Bible, and the White Man had the land." What the white man really had was two sets of values, both of which he conveniently but sincerely embraced at different times of the week—or even the day, or the hour.

Similarly, Karl Marx, the messianic father of "scientific socialism," could devote his intellect to the alleviation of human suffering, yet shun his own son Freddy by actually giving him away to working-class parents, to live as a common laborer and die a pauper. And United States President Thomas Jefferson could pen a constitution proclaiming all men divinely free, yet keep slaves himself—and father a child by one.

Or consider the recent slew of zealots who chose to martyr themselves for Islam by converting hijacked jets into lethal incendiary bombs and massacring some three thousand innocent civilians who happened to be working within the Twin Towers of the World Trade Center. On the night before this so-called "holy mission," in total disregard for the Islam faith, some of these misguided missionaries not only got drunk on Vodka at a local watering hole, but also enjoyed the services of comely Western lap-dancers.

Philosopher Thomas Macaulay saw the paradox a century ago and noted that "If a man should act, for one day, on the supposition that all the people about him were influenced by the religion which they professed, he would find himself ruined by night."

5. OUR VALUES ENABLE US TO MANUFACTURE OPINIONS ON EVERYTHING.

We don't actually need to *know* anything to hold an opinion.

In fact, as the character Archie Bunker demonstrated in the hit television series, *All in the Family*, the more ignorant the man the more he delights in his opinions on everything.

Where do these opinions come from? Obviously, they come from our underlying values.

Our values permit us to *manufacture* opinions on any subject, regardless of how little we may know about it.

So, in a discussion, we can produce an endless stream of semi-programmed responses on just about any subject—motherhood, lovers, apple pie, violence, justice, communism, godliness, newspapers, money, art, literature. The list truly is endless. Rarely do these opinions bear much relationship to reality. They're like the stopped clock, right twice a day at best.

6. WE BELIEVE THAT OUR VALUES ARE THE ONLY VALUES WORTH HOLDING.

The mark of the mental prisoner lies in "thinking" that his constellation of values—his perspective or *mind*-set, and nobody else's—is some kind of holy writ.

That's why he "chose" those particular values, right?

Jimmy Hoffa once remarked, "I may have my faults but being wrong ain't one of them."

Where their options are concerned, most people feel much the same way—strongly.

Sometimes they may hedge a little, saying, "Well, that's my opinion, and I'm entitled to it."

In so doing they fail to appreciate that the idea of being *entitled* to an opinion is just one more example of fuzzy thinking.

Sure, in the United States of America, anyway, one has a *legal* right to hold and express any opinion, no matter how silly. But in the realm of ideas, logic ultimately rules, so the notion that all opinions are equally valid is merely a nice example of a wrongheaded value judgment.

7. WE WANT TO CONVERT OTHER PEOPLE TO OUR VALUES.

If TV evangelists are telling the truth, then why are they always shouting? Like so many crusaders, the TV evangelist raises his voice because he's actually unsure that what he's saying is true. Converting people to his beliefs convinces him that what he's saying *is* true—and that, of course, keeps him happy. This is typical of all zealots, propagandists, and professional crusaders. It was certainly true of my dinner guest, the law professor, for whom it became a matter of necessity to press a federal judge to accept the notion that John Quincy Adams was, for at least one period in his life, anyway, a traitor to the cause of free speech. No one, of course, is keener to produce a new convert than the recent convert. It's like being the subject of a practical joke: our first reaction is annoyance, but then we look around for someone else to trick. The situation can become more frightening than humorous, however, when an offspring or friend embraces the beliefs of a religious zealot.

8. WE WILL FIGHT RATHER THAN SURRENDER OUR BELIEFS.

Most wars are, indeed fought over so-called moral beliefs. We kill for peace, for liberty, equality, fraternity—for the sake of humankind.

Were the hijackers who destroyed the World Trade Center any crazier than the idiot who concocted the line that justified unseemly killings in Vietnam? "To save the village we must destroy it."

The "holy wars" that claimed so many lives are about one set of godly beliefs being worth more than another.

Of course, if you *can* win the battle for the mind, then you may not need to go to war at all. Consider, for example, the Iranian revolution.

The late Shah of Iran commanded one of the world's mightiest military arsenals, yet he was overthrown by an eighty-year-old religious fanatic wielding only words, Xerox paper, and homemade tape recordings. Khomeini took charge of his people without firing a single bullet— he did it by winning the space between their ears.

But logic played no part, of course—he merely swung the Iranians back to his conception of "traditional Islamic values." Effectively, he turned the key that locks the unthinking person into the prison of parental programming.

The Bin Laden phenomenon added a delightful twist. Disciples of that misguided guru were taught that their religion *required* them to kill Americans and Jews. And that if the aforesaid disciples martyred themselves in the course of that holy mission they would awake in paradise to savor seventy beautiful virgins.

Englishmen scoff at the naiveté of Muslims taken in by such bromides, yet admire and would presumably respond to the battle cry of Shakespeare's Henry V:

We few, we happy few, we band of brothers,
for he today who sheds his blood with me shall be my brother.
Be he ne'er so vile, this day shall gentle his condition,
and gentlemen in England now abed shall think themselves accursed,
and hold their manhoods cheap whiles any speaks
that fought with us upon St Crispans Day.

Hey, brotherhood! A belief worth dying for, right? Well, as Osama bin Laden himself might have responded, "Yes and, uh, no." Or, "Yes for you, and no for me."

9. EVEN THE SMARTEST AMONG US STEADFASTLY DEFEND CRAZY VALUES.

Pointing to logical flaws in a person's core beliefs rarely evokes change. That's because even the smartest among us can't quickly adjust conditioning of which, by definition, we're unconscious. We're *compelled* to disagree, even though we truly don't know why. You'd think that intelligence, education, and experience would give people the capacity to rethink and remake their values. In fact, in just about any argument between "intelligent" people, the protagonists simply proffer increasingly sophisticated rationalizations while never budging an emotional or intellectual inch. Just listen to the talking heads on any political commentary channel any day of the week to see this syndrome acted out. Expecting logic to change values is, anyway, a little naive since value judgments have little or no basis in fact. We merely believe what we want to believe, and hear only those "facts" that support our beliefs.* However well intentioned, the introduction of "logic" into a discussion of values generally signals the opening dance in a three-item concert.

> **The Tape-Measure Tango.** An earnest talking head on a television show offered up the contention that presidential wannabe Al Gore "exaggerates so often he can't tell the truth without lying." A cheap shot, of course, and, since the remark reveals that the windbag who made the remark is equally prone to stretching the truth, it is self-defeating, too. Such exaggeration is something of a universal human problem. I mean, we all do it, right? But are we *really* lying? No, not really. We're merely invoking a "logical" process—rationalization—that resembles an elastic tape measure, which we stretch and twist in order to make it accommodate anything we want it to. And because the process of stretching the tape measure is unconscious, we rarely realize what we are doing. In consequence, we are very sincere in our deceptions and may even believe we are holding up the truth for all to see. But it is not *the* truth—it is simply *our* truth. A *New York Times* interview with the late John Lennon and his wife, Yoko Ono, nicely illustrates the point. The couple explained that they were socialists, even though their income ran into tens of millions and they owned several lavish homes plus a private jet. "There is no doubt that we are living in a capitalist world," Ms. Ono elucidated. "In order to change the world you have to take care of yourself first." But of course! In order to be good socialists, the Lennons needed to hang on to their capital. For us, the point is that Ms. Ono was undoubtedly telling the truth *as she saw it.* She *is* a socialist—but only inside her skull.

> **The Silent Waltz.** An old man who was partially deaf literally turned off his hearing aid whenever he was losing an argument with his

---

*The "Foxx experiment" is as nice an example as I know of this truly universal human foible. An auditorium of students listened to what they thought was a lecture by a distinguished authority. In fact, the fellow, "Doctor Foxx," gave a rambling, jargon-loaded speech that was actually meaningless. First his argument was radical, then it was conservative. The final effect was that he said nothing. Later, the students were polled as to the "Doctor's" perspective. The radical students said he was radical, the conservative students said he was conservative. Everyone agreed he had been both impressive and persuasive.

wife. Most of us do much the same even though our hearing is perfect. Our minds turn themselves off and the Silent Waltz commences. We enter a kind of trance, in which the mind simply doesn't hear whatever unwelcome arguments are being proffered. Research reveals that, when reading correspondence, the brain takes longer to comprehend bad news than good news. The fact is that the brain always attempts to reject bad news—including bad news in the form of other people's differing opinions. The paradox, however, is that, before the bad news can be rejected, it must be read or heard and comprehended. This process gives some idea of why we consistently overrate the worth of our judgments.

➤ **The Flight of the Bumblebee.** If pressed too far, we can resolve the conflict by becoming bellicose. We put on a grim mask and seek to dominate the discussion by talking quickly, raising our voices, pointing our fingers, and going on—and on and on—at length, refusing to let the other person make his points or answer our arguments. If this fails there are two ways out. First, like Berry we angrily buzz from the room with our hands over our ears. Ultimately, however, we might contemplate something infinitely more stinging. Well, I mean, we're entitled to our beliefs, aren't we? How dare you call me a hypocrite! There, you devil, take that! One of the more famous examples of such behavior occurred at a gathering of the literati. Hypersensitive novelist Norman Mailer punched the hyper-arrogant playwright Gore Vidal in the nose. Vidal came back with a memorable quip: "Poor Norman, words failed him, as usual."

10. WE PRIZE THE PARADOX THAT LOCKS THE BOX OF THE MIND.

Ultimately, there's a delicious paradox that locks the box of the mind. I call it the *Paradox of Values*.

The Paradox of Values lies in cherishing what we perceive to be a sacred right to hold invalid and conflicting values.

We do so because we think our "principles" make us free.

In truth, however, the opposite is the case.

Our values and beliefs compel us to live our lives in accordance with illusions—*and thereby imprison us.*

So, we think we are in charge of our lives, when, in fact, we are prisoners of our thinking processes.

Like the elephant, our beliefs deny us the capacity to perceive the true reality. We become tethered to thought patterns that lock the door to true freedom.

The final irony is that we will fight for the right to remain in jail.

William Shakespeare showed a profound understanding of the link between value systems and prisons in the following verbal jousting between Hamlet and a couple of courtiers:

Hamlet: What have you, my good friends, deserved at the hands of Fortune that she sends you to my prison hither?
Guildenstern: Prison, my lord?
Hamlet: Denmark's a prison.
Rosenkrantz: Then the world is one.
Hamlet: A goodly one; in which there are many confines, wards, and dungeons, Denmark being one of the worst.
Rosenkrantz: We think not so, my lord.
Hamlet: Why, then, 'tis none to you, for there is nothing either good or bad but thinking makes it so. To me it is a prison.

True indeed, and the paradox of values that locks people in so many confines, wards, and dungeons is pivotal to most people's thinking— which is true regardless of intelligence level or education. If we now examine a further crucial concept—one that I call the psychic contract—we can immediately see why so many good citizens find themselves trapped in wasted lives.

The Pact that Spells Prison—The Psychic Contract

I was working in an ad agency when I expressed admiration for the work of a fifty-year-old copywriter. He discounted the compliment. "Oh, I'm not really a copywriter," he said. "I'm a short story writer."

"Wonderful!" I replied. "What have you published?"

"Well, I send my work to *The Atlantic Monthly*."

"Oh, that's great!"

"Well, they've never actually *published* anything," he said. "But at least I got this very nice note from them." He fished into his pocket and extracted an envelope containing an impersonal dog-eared rejection letter on *Atlantic Monthly* stationery. "Look at the bottom," he urged. I took my eyes to the bottom of the page to discover that someone had scribbled in thick blue pencil, "You came close this time."

"They get thousands of submissions, so can you *imagine* how close I must have come?" he said plaintively, as much to himself as to me.

My colleague, no longer young, was looking backwards. He was also decidedly ambivalent about the near success that he seemed to realize would mark the zenith of his accomplishments. Some in the agency called him a loser. I wasn't so sure. He had, after all, confronted the empty white page. He had both written his story and risked rejection by sending it off. Better to have loved and lost, perhaps.

The key to spotting winners and losers, however, is to appreciate that most children embrace the values of their parents, and, before getting out of their teens strike a *psychic contract*, whereby success in life is tacitly defined as marginally outperforming one's parents in terms of income or status.

Parental expectations are crucial here. As parents, we are generally keen for our children to emulate us, but not embarrass us. And, of course, Carl Jung observed that nothing has a greater effect on a child than the unrealized ambitions of its parents. We want our children to make good on our dreams. The parental expectations generally crystallize into what I call the *Prime Parental Injunction* or *PPIN*—an oft-repeated instruction delivered from the parent to the child that becomes a vital guiding force in the selection of lifestyle and goals.

The process of fixing the contract is mostly unconscious, which explains why most people dedicate their lives to fulfilling the psychic contract, even as they argue that they are doing no such thing.

On a conscious plane, the psychic contract manifests as a *culminating event*, or a crucial, later-life concrete milestone that signals ultimate success or failure.

The specific culminating event varies from person to person. culminating events might include being appointed to a particular role—chief executive, professor, lead violinist, senior partner, whatever. Other culminating events might include founding a business, accumulating a million dollars, getting a child into a fine college, paying off a mortgage, having a book published, and so on.

A *winner*, in terms of the psychic contract, is someone who makes good on his promise. He sets a goal, commits himself to it, and ultimately achieves it. His covenant or dream may be to run a sub-four-minute mile, or write a great novel, or become a professor at Harvard, or direct a great corporation. If he achieves his aim, he is a winner.

If, in the pursuit of those particular goals, a person finishes barely breaking five minutes for the mile, getting published by a vanity house, becoming a corporate trainer, or managing a hamburger franchise, then this person clearly is a *loser*.

If that person runs the mile in four minutes, ten seconds, is appointed associate professor at Yale, becomes a vice-president, or writes a thriller, he could well be described as an *at-leaster*—not a loser, but not a winner either.

The key point is this: winning or losing—or whatever—merely involve, making good on a *mental* contract. That being the case, one could revise the contract and become an instant winner merely by running a six-minute mile, playing a tin whistle, holding onto a safe job, or becoming a scout instructor.

In reality, however, most people fail to make this mental adjustment. Instead, they simply follow the voice of conscience, become imprisoned in the cage of values, and perform what they imagine to be their duty, which is to say, to attempt to fulfill the terms of the psychic contract.

For some lucky people, the goals set by the parent are totally in accord with their own wishes. Such a person can still wind up a loser. The culminating event merely needs to be set too high for the child's talents. This is a common problem among would-be achievers. The key to happiness in such cases is to adjust the psychic contract, but, as noted, the mind itself blocks serious contemplation of this option.

These underlying problems with the way the mind works—or the way we unwittingly use it—don't stop with the psychic contract. Our vision may also become colored by the tendency to view the world through the prism of an emotional state. Let's see how that works.

The Wounded Child Syndrome

Psychologist Eric Berne, author of *Games People Play*, noted that in our everyday lives we all tend to swing between three states or modes—adult, child, and parent.

- In our adult state, we think calmly and rationally, picking our way through ideas to find the means to attain whatever might be the goal at hand.

- In the child state, we think and behave like children, playing, dreaming, and seeking affection, praise, and pleasure.

- In the parent mode, we assume the role of the stern, punishing, omniscient parent, *the* authority upon *all* subjects.

In fact, many people get stuck in one of these three modes, and all their thinking becomes one-dimensional.

As we've already seen, most inmates were emotionally injured during childhood. The next thing to note is that *emotional wounds can arrest intellectual growth*. Hoping to protect his early wounds, the injured child—of whatever chronological age—becomes trapped in infantile patterns of perception. He fails to realize, consciously anyway, that he is merely attempting to deny underlying feelings of inferiority. He can be likened to an infant, who, if left unattended, might burn the house down. To protect the child and the home, society hires professional baby-sitters—prison guards, actually—and incarcerates the recalcitrant juvenile in a so-called correctional institution. A similar syndrome affects a great many apparently free citizens. They, however, merely check themselves into rather more appealing prisons.

So, then, these, in a nutshell, are the reasons why our thinking processes can imprison us:

- the paradox of values can turn the mind into a cage;

- the psychic contract can impair our ability to choose to pursue the winning life of our own dreams;

- an injured sense of self-esteem can lock us into a fixed and faulty perspective on the world, leaving us to view the world through the faulty prism of an infantile value system.

But does all this really affect our actual behavior? You can bet your life on that, and the odds are that you already have.

CHAPTER 4

The Iron Ball Tagged <u>0</u>
& Why Your Maneuvers Are Ineffective

That deed is not well done
which one regrets when it is done,
and the result of which one
experiences with a tearful face.

—Buddha

"Hey John—"
A hand falls on my shoulder.

I'm halfway through the current semester and about to begin another session. I turn into the forty-year-old face of Mercado. He's usually resentful and negative—but not today.

"You've changed my life!" he exclaims. "I'm suddenly seeing things I never saw before."

Transformations can be swift. The right idea—or even a phrase or a word—can turn on the light. Mercado's upbeat voice and upright demeanor suggest that he might indeed have undergone such a metamorphosis.

"That's great news, Mercado. But the real test will come in a couple of months when they let you back out onto the street. You're a bright guy, but you still have to figure out a way to support yourself, right?"

He momentarily contemplates the question, then plunges right on. "Hey, listen John. You've totally changed me, from the inside out. I'll tell that to *anyone*—even if I come back to Rikers a hundred times."

Mercado is utterly sincere and what he's saying is more profound than amusing, actually. He really has learned something special. But for better reasons than he probably realizes, he's doubtful that his new knowledge will make the journey from his brain to his legs.

He's like one of those weekend golfers who pays a professional to tune his game prior to the club championship. He gets everything straight in his head and he might even hit some nice balls from the

61

practice tee. But when the pressure of a real match comes on, he simply forgets everything and regresses to his old ways.

Mercado's problems don't spring from his inability to hit a golf ball. His difficulties stem from his inability to fit into society. The why of that, as we've seen, comes down to neurotic feelings of inferiority. But there's a further point: ultimately, most such feelings spring from unhappy childhood relationships with authority. As psychologist Erich Fromm observes, "The scars left from the child's defeat in the fight against irrational authority are to be found at the bottom of every neurosis." Which leads directly to the prison of obedience.

The Prison of Obedience

The parable of the prodigal son tells of a rebellious younger son who deciding that his father is a know-nothing, asks for his inheritance, and then stalks off to seek his fortune in the wider world. He engages in "riotous living," falls upon hard times, and ultimately winds up as a lowly servant on a farm, feeding swill to swine. At this point, he sees the light, realizes that his father was a good provider, goes back home and begs his father to take him back, even as a common laborer. The father, delighted that his defiant son has been freed from the prison of immaturity and unrealism, orders his servants to bring robes, shoes, and jewels for the reformed rebel, and then to kill the fatted calf and prepare a feast in honor of the son's return.

The story of the prodigal son can be read on several levels. First, it is the story of just about every thinking person's enlightenment, and certainly that of virtually every prison inmate I ever met. It is about making mistakes, escaping the prison of wishful thinking, seeing the world through adult eyes, and consciously choosing to join the contributing members of society.

The parable relates to my discussion with José. The prodigal son's perceptions did not accord with reality, so reality became his teacher. Shakespeare has Regan make the same point in King Lear: "O sir, to willful men, the injuries that they themselves procure must be their schoolmasters."

The elder of the two sons, returning from the fields, is irked by the hero's welcome accorded to his sibling and runs to the father. "I've served you faithfully and obediently for many years but you never gave me a calf to make merry with my friends," he says, "yet the instant my brother returns from wasting your money with harlots, you kill the fatted calf for him." The elder son doesn't really want a feast to call his own. But he is miffed by the whole situation. First, he's unhappy at the prospect of having to share profits with the errant homecoming brother. More important, however, is his desire to retain the preferred status he'd hoped to win by virtue of conforming to his father's expectations.

In the most obvious interpretation, the father of the parable can be any number of people, including one's own parents, one's true self, society, nature, or one's God. The idea is that this person—this higher power—is always there for us.

The parable beautifully illustrates how the entire family has been imprisoned by "the prison of obedience." French philosopher Rousseau famously observed that "man is born free yet is everywhere in chains." In both business and life, those chains are all too often the chains of authority. Children must learn to get along with authority, then outgrow the need for it. Authority figures must learn how to wield authority in such a way that they can ultimately give it up. Until that happens, life can be a trial for everyone. Consider, for example, the unholy trinity locked in the prison of obedience. I call them Demandio, Obedio, and Contrario.

DEMANDIO

> *Authority without wisdom is like a heavy axe*
> *without an edge, fitter to bruise than to polish.*
> *—Anne Bradstreet*

In the parable of the prodigal son, Demandio would be the father. As a successful farmer and substantial employer, he was probably also used to having his way, and like most small-time entrepreneurs, opinionated and autocratic.

As a father, however, Demandio's job entailed more than merely directing his sons to do his bidding. His role was to teach them how to become emotionally, intellectually, and financially self-reliant.

Instead, Demandio established the same psychic contract for both sons—stay on the farm and follow in father's footsteps—and that wound up creating problems for everyone.

One son became an out-and-out rebel, and the other became a stunted clone. At the close of the parable, both sons regressed to the original contract and remained totally dependent upon the old man—so the inference is pretty clear: the father was either a poor teacher or insensitive to his sons' needs.

Demandios abound in business. They can direct an organization but are intolerant of any staff member who fails to bend the knee. The result is that the achievers leave and the conformists stay. This is good news for Demandio, for it leaves him without a rival and he can kid himself that he really is indispensable and therefore has no option but to cling to power.

OBEDIO

There is truth in the high opinion that in
so far as a man conforms he ceases to exist.
—Max Eastman

Obedio would be the stay-on-the-farm son who becomes the stunted clone. Such individuals mistake conformity for adulthood. They hope to avoid having to fend for themselves in a threatening world by exchanging autonomy and freedom for security and structure. They hope to be carried to success in life by virtue of following their leader's orders. If things go wrong, however, they quickly shift all blame to their guru. Obedios look like team players, but since they have given up their minds, obeisance is their only option and true teamwork is impossible.

American slavery systematically and cruelly created a population of Obedios whose descendants one readily encounters in prison. This generation of Obedios were denied the opportunity to learn how to earn an income, so they joined a gang or stole or attempted to deal drugs—or all of the above.

Obedios might seem relatively harmless, impotent, even. In fact, they're highly dangerous both to themselves and to others, for their minds and bodies can be snatched up by unscrupulous leaders, thereby creating an enormous potential for evil. Adolf Hitler persuaded Nazi

Obedios to incinerate six million Jews. When ultimately brought to justice, the manager of that particular operation offered the classic Obedio alibi, "I was merely following orders." Similarly, cult leader "Reverend" Jim Jones persuaded his rag-tag bunch of forlorn Obedios to kill themselves by drinking poison-laced Kool-Aid, and Osama bin Laden successfully tempted a team of spoiled-rotten, spiritually hungry Obedios to sacrifice their lives in order to murder thousands of innocents.

CONTRARIO

> *I don't like authority, at least*
> *I don't like other people's authority.*
> —*A.C. Benson*

Contrario is the rebellious son.

Mavericks can make outstanding executives, but only if their imagination is authentic and they possess the discipline to work without structure—but this, for sure, Contrarios cannot do.

In fact, though they loudly protest the opposite, Contrarios are equally as obedient as their conformist brothers. The difference is merely this: a Contrario's programming is all backwards. If his master asks him to advance he reflexively halts or shifts to reverse. He imagines that he is exerting free will, but in fact he possesses none. His mind is never his own for his leader supplies his motivation.

Contrario's contrariness is merely *negative obedience*. Contrarios obey Newtonian law and exert an equal and opposite force to any expectation others might have for them. They waste untold energy responding to their masters when they should be responding to their situations. They are late when they should be early, disruptive when they should cooperate, zombies if called upon to socialize.

Contrario is compelled to obstruct the will of the group or its leader and, being a hyper-obedient slave for whom there is no other choice, will sabotage himself rather than cooperate.

Most of the Contrarios in my prison classes—where they are very well represented, indeed—are highly intelligent, yet in an irony more depressing than delicious, their compulsive contrariness consistently gets them into trouble with the very authorities upon whom they are totally dependent.

Contrario's tragedy is that he turns his cleverness upon himself by dedicating his entire intellect to supporting the mistaken certainty that he is tough-minded and autonomous.

Obsolete Grappling Styles

The parable of the prodigal demonstrates that each of us finds a way to win the affection we need as we struggle to survive childhood. In that struggle we develop a pattern of behaviors that distill into a *grappling style*. The style may not always be efficient, and it might not work for everybody, but somehow we make it work for us, and soon enough, it becomes an ingrained aspect of our personality. In his autobiography, Malcolm X describes the process perfectly:

> I learned early that crying out in protest could accomplish things. My older brothers and sister had started school when, sometimes, they would come and ask for a buttered biscuit or something and my mother would tell them, impatiently, no. But I would cry and make a fuss until I got what I wanted. I remember well how my mother asked me why I couldn't be a nice boy like Wilfred; but I would think to myself that Wilfred, for being so nice and quiet, often stayed hungry. So, early in life, I had learned that if you want something, you had better make some noise.

Malcolm's petulant grappling style attracted trouble in his teens but he ultimately honed it in his fight for civil rights. Wilfred didn't fare so well.

Birth-order psychology tells us that a person is naturally conditioned to maintain his or her place in the family—and continue to earn the respect, attention, and approval of other family members—then, later, of the world at large.

In fact, as we saw with Demandio, Obedio, and Contrario, many supposed adults become trapped in grappling styles that are obsolete. They live in the past and continue to fight—or charm, or woo, or please, or impress—childhood ghosts. Consider Alonzo, for example.

"As a kid, I stole a bike," says Alonzo.

"Why did you do that?"

"I needed a bike. I figured I was as smart and just as deserving as anybody, but I could see that no one was going to give me a bike. And there was no way I could get one. So there was no choice. I just stole one. I felt good about doing it, too. It was a great bike. It made a great impression. People looked at me differently."

These days Alonzo's serving time for stealing cars. What he hasn't quite realized is that the grappling style that enabled him to own a bike is not only obsolete, it's also getting him into serious trouble. He's a savvy, intelligent, prepossessing thirty-year-old Contrario who could earn just about any reasonable credential he set his mind to, and then go on to build a wonderful life. Why doesn't he do this? Well, first, because he's a wounded child who simply doesn't believe himself capable of earning a living within the law. Second, he's trying to apply his old grappling style to the entirely different demands of his current situation. In a crazy kind of way, it's working for him, too. He's getting his three-hots-and-a-cot, and he's excused from having to worry about his wife and kids. After all, he asks himself, what can I possibly do to help anybody from in here? He's also getting attention by acting up in my class, pointing out how terribly unfair the world has been, not just to him, but also to everyone like him.

Ultimately, an obsolete grappling style produces a frustrated individual looking for something or someone to blame, an artificial means of anesthetizing an unhappy psyche, or a way of escaping his predicament, at no matter what cost to himself.

INMATES SHACKLED BY OBSOLETE GRAPPLING STYLES WITHIN THE PRISON OF OBEDIENCE

The Shackles of Rivalry

The final point I'd like to draw from the parable of the prodigal son is that sibling rivalry is something of a junior prison that can set the foundation for a lifetime of incarceration.

In the parable, when Obedio sullenly demands to know why the calf should be sacrificed to celebrate the return of his errant brother, the father somewhat misses the point with an all-too-rational answer, "You are always with me and all I have is yours. It is right to celebrate, for your brother has effectively returned from the dead."

But, hey, *that's* the problem—the troublesome brother *is* back from the dead, bigger, better, and brighter than ever. This is bad news indeed for the stunted stay-at-home sibling, who would infinitely prefer the rival for his father's affection dead.

The Old Testament story of Cain and Abel drives the point home with absolute clarity. Cain kills his brother, Abel, out of jealousy, then attempts to hide the crime with the infamous question, "Am I my brother's keeper?"

Harold S. Kushner, in his wonderful book *How Good Do We Have to Be?*, profoundly observes that sibling rivalry lies in the pervasive childhood fear that *there will not be enough love to go around.*

What the child does not understand, of course, is that parents simply cannot love their children equally—and, fortunately, do not need to. Instead, they love each of them *uniquely.*

The father probably underwent his own transformation after having his younger son walk out on him. It seems a safe bet that he loved both sons uniquely, prizing the loyalty of one and the rebelliousness of the other. He nonetheless welcomed the ultimate transformation of the rebel son and doubtless hoped for similar growth in the passive-aggressive brother.

Delegates within my prison class are quick to draw lessons from this parable. They know the enlightenment that comes from the realization that their injuries, unrealism, and behavioral patterns are the root causes of their imprisonment. They reenter the world transformed, yet upon release they suffer resentment and envy from those less enlightened—those people who never went astray, and therefore don't really understand the lessons that what these days we call *recovery* can teach.

For the sake of clarity, let's summarize the process by which so many people become ensnared in the related prisons of poor grappling styles, unhealthy rivalries, and low self-esteem.

- ➤ As children, we lack the capacity to generate self-approval, and so we feel the need to compete with siblings for the approval and affection of our parents. As self-esteem develops we escape that prison by becoming less dependent upon parental approval until we finally do not need it at all, or not so much of it, anyway. Ideally, in adulthood we confer affection and approval upon others.

- ➤ There's a special problem for the person whose self-esteem becomes impaired, however. Not only can he not escape the prison of sibling rivalry, the human mind being what it is, *he sees virtually every person in his milieu as a rival for love and affection*, a competitor to be ousted or outdone by any means necessary.

- ➤ Then, alas, just as such a person's thinking processes are impaired by a shaky sense of self-esteem, so too is his actual behavior. He cannot conceive of an even playing field and so he cannot compete on one. He cannot contribute as an equal so he finds another way to get the spotlight off others and onto himself, thereby maintaining the preferred child status. So what does he do then? *He sounds the bugle and advances to the rear.*

How to Sound the Bugle and Advance to the Rear

To sound the bugle and advance to the rear involves the use of an obsolete grappling style to catch everyone's attention by doing something both self-aggrandizing and counterproductive.

The prodigal son sounded the bugle by demanding his inheritance, then he advanced to the rear by running away and punishing his father by wasting the old man's hard-earned money on riotous living. His obedient brother sounded the bugle by yessing the old man to death, and advanced to the rear by relinquishing his own mind.

Others are forced not only to gaze upon the bugler's infantile behavior, they are also called upon to pamper him, tend to his daily needs, and soothe his anger at the world and the way that it has treated him.

Buglers abound in prison. They sounded the bugle with angry declarations of victimhood—in which there is both more and less truth than they quite understand—and then advanced to the rear by engaging in criminal behavior and getting themselves caught. There are many ways to play the bugle and advance to the rear—some obvious, some subtle.

➤ Bob was a gifted golfer, a guy who could hit a golf ball as far and as straight as anyone in the world. Despite his tremendous advantage off the tee, however, he consistently missed the cut for major national events. His first problem was that the shots from sixty yards in let him down. His second problem was that he never practiced them. He got all the attention he needed by failing. For Bob, this was a better option than exposing his wounded child to the further possibility of further failure.

➤ Geoff, on parole from prison, attended a series of night classes. This was a good idea save for one thing. It was now impossible for him to make it home in time to meet his evening curfew. A small thing, according to Geoff, but not to the police officer who, noting Geoff's furtiveness, asked to see some ID. That Geoff had violated parole was immediately revealed. He was rearrested and returned to prison—where he called me to lament the fact that he had been "victimized merely for trying to better myself."

➤ Rico, a gifted public speaker with a razor-sharp intellect, was selected to represent the Rikers three-man team against a group of outstanding attorneys from outside the prison system. In prison classes Rico was always a standout, though, unfortunately, extremely arrogant. He liked to pit his intellect against other inmates in order to ridicule them. Now that he'd been selected to the prison debate team, however, he'd be facing his equals—at the least—and the thought of failure in front of his classmates proved too much for him to bear. He sounded the bugle by finding fault with the selection process and then advanced to the rear by withdrawing from the debate "on principle."

➤ Henry, a newly appointed chief executive in over his head, sounded the bugle by demanding the entire top floor of the corporate headquarters for a new private office. Then he advanced to the rear by installing a Caligulan lavatory into which he disappeared for hours at a time, emerging only for golf games at his outrageously expensive country club.

In fact, the corporate world is rife with so-called executives imprisoned by obsolete grappling styles. In that ethos, however, the term is an "ineffective management style." The style works reasonably well at one level of the organization, but becomes obsolete at another. Rather than adjusting to the new situation, the imprisoned executive instead develops sophisticated bugle-sounding and advancing-to-the-rear devices, such as:

> **Doing the bureaucratic shuffle.** First, explaining that all problems must be treated in serial order, then assigning the current one to the bottom of the pile. Sounding a clarion call for indefinite delay: "We must crawl before we walk, walk before we run," and "Haste makes waste." Using double-talk: If this is true, we do this, except in this or that circumstance, when we do the opposite, but not in the south, except when the seasons are appropriate. If enough confusion can be created, perhaps the problem will be forgotten. Portentously delegating the problem to a committee and waiting—and waiting, and waiting—for it to make a recommendation. Seeking an answer in the book. If no answer is to be found, then, of course, no action can be taken.

> **Passing the buck.** Avowing that the problem belongs in "someone else's province." Inducing the boss to commit herself on how to handle the problem; if the solution is wrong, the problem is hers. Practicing "democratic-participative" management: delegate the problem to a subordinate; perhaps *he* can find a way to untie the Gordian knot. Calling in a consultant, an accountant, or a lawyer, or some other expert to "make sure we're on solid ground"—then scapegoating him if the recommendations are wrong. Becoming "too busy," too mired in meaningless detail, to consider the problem.

> **Citing a sound reason to flee the office.** One favorite is to book a round-the-world flight to meet with suppliers or prospective clients. No one will be able to reach the incompetent on a plane, and, of course, with any kind of good luck, someone on the ground will find a solution, somehow.

➤ **Becoming ill.** Developing a psychogenic illness such as a heart condition, blinding migraine headaches, colitis, or ulcers. A variant on this is to develop an alcohol problem or commit a felony and get sent to jail. Both stratagems offer immediate gratification on five levels. They are:

1. **Remove the bugler from the scene of the stress.** Executives will advance to the rear by becoming confined to bed, and then the doctor will prescribe a protracted holiday. Prisoners will be confined to cots and "rehabilitated" for months or even years.

2. **Shield him from the realization of his unwillingness to deal with the issues of life.** The essence of a defense mechanism is that it protects the sufferer from the perception that it is in fact a defense mechanism. Thus, the incompetent believes that his ulcer—or his unjust society—is rendering him incapable of doing his job. The truth is exactly the opposite; he is incapacitated precisely because he is incapable of addressing life's challenges.

3. **Command sympathy and attention from colleagues.** One cannot be blamed, surely, for getting an ulcer. No, of course not. What one is entitled to expect is understanding and special treatment. The same is often said—especially in Manhattan, and especially by career criminals—of getting arrested and sent to jail.

4. **Punish him.** The superego that punished him with anxiety now substitutes ulcers—or a prison sentence—for apprehension. This is part of the price, albeit on an unconscious level, that the incompetent exacts of himself for being absent from work.

5. **Punish his superiors.** The reprimand is relatively subtle. The words may be unspoken but the message is unmistakable: You've made me work so hard for you, and now look at what you've done to me.

THE ULTIMATE PRODIGAL

I stood on lower Fifth Avenue and watched the Twin Towers burn, crumble, and fall. Later, a friend asked me what I thought of it all. What I think, I replied, is that Mr. Bin Laden has a serious self-esteem problem.

To my nonsurprise, a week or so later, a supermarket tabloid* reported that the teenage Osama did indeed suffer an injury to his self-esteem: either a kidney condition or a disease called Sporadic Kallmans Syndrome stunted the growth of his genitalia. Then, so the story goes, a girl from Chicago whom the teenage Osama was attempting to seduce mocked the offending equipment. Bear in mind also that Osama was the prodigal son in a family of fifty or so siblings, which is quite an emotional burden to bear, and that in the tradition of the prodigal, he fled his homeland of Saudi Arabia with an obscene inheritance of $60 million, a sum guaranteed to further stunt such a person's value system.

Another person—a mature adult, actually—might have invested at least some of that money in a direct, positive contribution to humankind.

Instead, Osama sounded the bugle with a litany of hate against the free world, then advanced to the rear by financing mayhem and destruction.

After seeing the Twin Towers fall, I lingered on Fifth Avenue as subdued throngs of well-mannered people emerged and trekked uptown. What struck me most was the ethnic mix. No single group dominated. It was as diverse an entourage of blacks and Hispanics, Asians, Arabs, and whites as I have ever seen. The conclusion seemed clear: to make himself seem as big a man as his father, Contrario had unleashed his hapless band of Obedio brothers upon the world itself.

Osama bin Laden was effectively trapped in the prison of immaturity, unrealism, and destructive behavior. His subsequent lack of remorse—and his vindictive pleasure, in having inflicted pain—came as no surprise. Such overt denial is common among prison inmates. Numbed by horrendous early emotional injuries, they, too, try to even the score with violent criminal behavior. Victim Awareness classes help them peel the calluses from their damaged hearts and thereby regain consciousness and humanity. The ultimate payoff comes slowly in liberating feelings of guilt and remorse.

Yet there are some people who are too badly damaged to be helped.

---

*The Globe, Oct. 2, 2001, quoted as confirmed by Larry Johnson, former deputy director of counterterrorism at the U.S. State Department.

How to Land a Life Sentence

In all, it's a short hop from Plato's remark that the unexamined life is not worth living, to Thoreau's observation about most men living lives of quiet desperation. The idea that we have only one life to live—our own—and limited time to savor it can seem overwhelming to many. So instead of creating familial happiness and job fulfillment, they attempt to grapple with existence by following outworn scripts inherited from parents, various mentors or so-called heroes. There's nothing new under the sun, so such contracts are already recorded in biblical lore. Permit me to illustrate six such obsolete scripts and associated grappling styles.

1. THE NEVER

The Never is the script of those whose parents forbade them to take whatever they'd most like from life. Moses, for example, though chosen to lead his people to the Promised Land, was condemned by God never to enter it himself. Many apparently outstanding executives are caught in the same bind. They're instructed to spend their days *building an empire*, but are forbidden to taste the milk and honey their labors create.

Prison inmates commonly fall victim to related parental directives. "You'll never amount to anything," and "You'll never get out of jail."

Executive Nevers seldom enjoy any given moment. They are forever saying things like "I can't stay because I've just got to" or "I'd like to but" or "Got to run now."

Inmate Nevers are forever making excuses. For many the Never is justice—they're certain that they're "never gonna get any of that." And one way or another, they'll do whatever might be necessary to ensure that they never do.

A variant is the Never who has all the time in the world to talk about what he'd really like to be doing, but begins every sentence with "Yes, but" whenever a change of situation—career, domicile, lifestyle, or whatever—is suggested.

2. THE ALWAYS

The Always is followed by people programmed to spend their lives in the single-minded pursuit of a single career. Usually this means Following in Father's footsteps, perhaps even carrying the same family cross. Sometimes, however, the Always is being punished by parents piqued that their child chose not to follow Father. Then into the psychic contract is imprinted a damned-for-all-eternity clause that warns: "If that's what you want to do, then you just go right ahead and spend the rest of your life doing it—and we hope it makes you happy"— which really means, "we hope it makes you miserable." So, when Always scriptees aren't rebelling, they often spend a lifetime of quiet desperation earning a living, while wishing they were doing something else. If not most, then many middle-management "executives" are running on Always programs. "But at least," says the Always, "I've always got my career." Indeed.

"You'll always be a nobody," is the injunction engraved upon the brain cells of inmate versions of the Always. In consequence they see themselves destined always to be suffering and downtrodden, always unemployable or underemployed, or always in jail. Like the executive, they are scripted—emotionally and intellectually—to believe that this really is their lot in life.

The compulsive housewife, Martha, was an Always. Jesus chided her for failing to realize that there was more to life than getting stuck in a cleaning and worrying mode. In fact, Martha likely savored the reprimand. After all, her behavior caught the Messiah's attention, thereby winning Martha a moment of perverse pleasure. So she was luckier than most, for Always scriptees seldom experience any kind of fulfillment.

3. THE UNTIL

Untils are programmed to work hard for the deserved reward in order to earn salvation that will come in the form of a special sacrament when the Until has been rendered ready to receive it. Most professions are worked on this basis. The neophyte lawyer serves years as a drudge, then when adjudged "ready" is made junior partner—and works even harder. Thus she makes her way until, one fine day, she is appointed—wait for it!—full partner. O holy and happy scenario! Finally, the blessed Until gets to sit in judgment as to whether other supplicants will be allowed to collect *their* Untils.

Untils tend to spend their lives playing the game—that is, doing whatever is necessary to make good on the Until. What this really means is that Untils gradually acquire all of the values of the group that promises fulfillment of the Until. This is a pronounced feature of corporate life, where Until rituals are as clearly defined as in any monastery.

Pontius Pilate, an organization man from way back, was enrolled in an Until program. Collecting his Until denied him the option of setting an apparently innocent cult leader free, so he washed his hands of the matter. As any other Until would have. No career prospects otherwise.

Untils carry psychic calendars. They say, "By age thirty—or forty, fifty, sixty, or sixty-five—they should make me a . . ." Winners say, "I was the youngest person ever to be made a . . ." Hopefuls say, "Pretty soon now they ought to make me a . . ." The loser says, "They never made me a . . ." Poor bastard.

Actually the fulfillment of any Until program can leave the scriptee with only blank cards, no matter what its age. That is part of the pain of winning at almost anything, and why scriptees who've just made good on their Untils usually suffer feelings of intense emptiness.

The inmate version of the Until is starker and sadder. He's programmed by society and poverty to pursue a life of crime. After that, it's only a matter of time until he gets himself arrested. He hones his criminal skills in prison, builds an effective network of like-minded felons, and waits for the big Until, the date of release. Then he reapplies himself to his old ways, and it's only a matter of time until he's back in prison, counting the days on the calendar, praying for his next Until to fall due. Such a script can steal a lifetime without the Until ever quite realizing what has happened.

4. THE AFTER

The premise of the After is that pride goeth before a fall, and that having fun presages misery—so watch out. Afters are raised by voices that foresee trouble in every situation, and say things like: "If you climb that tree, you'll only fall and hurt yourself." So Afters obsess about the rainy day that's bound to be attracted by good weather. They believe cleaning the car makes dark clouds come. Eating in fine restaurants makes them sick. Pure pleasure scares the heaven out of them.

Afters seek maximum job security. they don't take any risks. Armed with a fat manual, Afters sometimes seem to do well as bureaucrats, auditors, or bankers—anything requiring traits like insecurity, paranoia, and conservatism.

Afters love the story of Jezebel, the archetypal good-time girl who came to a sticky end. They also like the story of Sodom and Gomorra, whose sinful ways provoked God's destruction of their cities. A certain Mr. and Mrs. Lot, however, had lived good lives, so God permitted them to flee, but warned them: Don't look back. They were all but home free, when Mrs. Lot took a backward peep and was turned into a pillar of salt, apparently an unpleasant way to go. The moral, as Afters know, is be on guard lest some transient pleasure attract God's wrath.

Afters say, "It's not a great job, but I'm building a pension." Or "I can't just wait to retire and get outta here."

Afters seldom break the law, being too frightened to do so. Instead they hang out in the visiting chambers, offering cautious counsel and earnest homilies to the regular inmates. Their brand of reform falls under the "scare 'em straight" rubric. Unfortunately, this well-intentioned advice tends to be more than a little simplistic, and often counterproductive. The inmate sees into the frightened heart of the essentially dour After, and makes the judgment that it might just be better to remain a rebel than to join the ranks of the mentally imprisoned Afters.

5. THE OVER-AND-OVER

This is the classic loser's program and it is common to all walks of life. Anyone carrying it is destined to fail, over and over and over again. The poisonous parental injunction is "You'll go on failing at everything."

Paradoxically, Over-and-Overs of all stripes are attracted to get-rich-quick schemes. Riches seldom result, though. Over-and-Overs don't really look for ways to win, but for ways to lose.

Judas, running an Over-and-Over program, sold his soul for thirty pieces of silver, then lost that reward along with his reputation and his life. The original Over-and-Over was Sisyphus, condemned eternally to roll a large stone up a mountain, then to have it roll back to the bottom.

Over-and-Over scriptees tell of how they "almost made it," how "It will be different this time."

Richard Nixon was a classic Over-and-Over. When he ran for the presidency in 1968 he actually said," "I've changed, I'm a new Nixon."

Then came Watergate. And you don't need me to tell you that Nixon both created and refused to destroy those White House tapes because they were his best chance of self-destruction. Lyndon Johnson had foreseen it all. "Nixon can be beaten," he said. "He's like a Spanish horse who runs faster than anyone for the first nine lengths and then turns around and runs backwards. He'll do something wrong in the end. He always does."

Over-and-Overs abound in prison. Indeed, a much-quoted statistic is that 80 percent of released inmates return within six months. The figures for those attending my class are dramatically better, I'm pleased to report. Just the same, every recidivist is a disappointment. Thirty-year-old Mike exemplifies the breed. He was an Over-and-Over with a ton of excuses, but, realistically, no one to blame. He was highly educated, strongly credentialed, very presentable, and Caucasian. But he just kept on committing exactly the same foolish crime—using his computer expertise to steal funds from subway turnstiles—then getting rearrested within mere yards of committing the crime and being returned to prison. Despite having already completed my class, he let no advice of any kind penetrate his arrogant defenses. This time he talked his way into my presence to ask if *he* might help me teach the current class. "Maybe I could use you as an anti-role-model, Mike. Sit right up front next to me, and I'll point you out as an Over-and-Over—you remember? A recidivist for whom, despite intelligence and advantage, until he comes to his senses, there's no hope—for he receives so much pleasure and attention from being in prison that he'd rather stay here than live a productive life."

6. THE LIMBO

The Limbo is really no program at all, but simply the state many people reach at the end of their lives when they retire—or are released—and are suddenly left without a script or the wherewithal to create one. At such a time the corporate scriptee collects a gold watch and becomes an automatic nonwinner, even if he seems to have been a winner up until that moment. The parental directive that got the scriptee this far, "Do what you're told and you'll be a big success when you retire," is not much use when retirement—the Great Until—actually arrives. At that time the Limbo, habituated to a life of prestructured time must suddenly write his own programs—and no one ever programmed him to do that. So the gold watch really is most appropriate, both as a symbol and as a tool that will be in use almost every moment of every day.

Limbos spend the balance of their days waiting for Godot, or playing Mahler's *Resurrection Symphony* and hoping. If they get together at reunions they say, "At least we didn't make any mistakes."

James, a highly intelligent, fifty-year-old African-American ex-offender with two degrees from a fine university, is a Limbo. He got out of jail and he didn't go back. That was the good news. The downside was that he couldn't figure out what to do with the rest of his life. You might think, as I did, that his education would open doors. In fact, his sense of self-esteem is so low that he believes himself a phony, a fraud improperly preferred by affirmative action. He's wrong, but doesn't want to hear it. Paradoxically, his credentials merely irk and demotivate him. He resents the lack of a plausible excuse for his predicament—which is, of course, that he's become a Limbo: a heretofore successful person, suddenly bereft of goals, and reduced to twiddling his thumbs—or, in James's case, smoking pot—to fill in the remainder of his days.

The Iron Ball Tagged O—In a Nutshell

By way of summary, then, the iron ball tagged O, is an Obsolete Grappling Style—an ingrained way of dealing with the world that worked in childhood but now thwarts our ability to respond appropriately to here-and-now issues of adult life. Soon enough, the obsolete grappling style takes over one's entire life, leaving us with outcomes that we would never choose for ourselves if we had the chance to think about it.

But why, really, can't we think about changing the OGS?

Well, that's a very good question—so let's contemplate the answer.

CHAPTER 5

The Illusion that Locks the 3 Iron Balls in Place & Why You Can't Escape

I saw the iron bars behind his eyes
      And instinctively reached for my pliers.
But he hid his face behind his hands:
      "Those posts are purposely in place," he cried,
    "To keep out thieves and liars."
        —Chandler Haste

Donald was a brilliant divisional executive earning a $400,000 salary and holding a couple of million dollars' worth of stock options. He was upbeat, savvy, and got on well with everyone. But he did a very foolish thing. He concocted false expense invoices of less than $10,000 a year. It took five years but finally it happened: the auditors twigged to his luminous trail. I'd personally evaluated Donald at the time of his appointment so I was keen to uncover why this outstanding executive would trip himself up. He certainly didn't do it for another paltry $10,000 a year. I went back to the notes of our interview along with the results of Donald's psychological testing. What immediately caught my eye was the occupation of Donald's now deceased father. He'd been a *bank examiner!* So, in Freudian terms anyway, Donald's behavior suddenly made sense. He'd been trying to replay an unhappy childhood. He'd been leaving clues to catch his father's eye. Donald wasn't aware of this—and since he didn't believe in "all that psychological mumbo-jumbo," he fell victim to the *illusion of autonomy.* He *thought* he knew what he was doing—whereas in reality he simply didn't have a conscious clue.

The ultimately inspiring life of Malcolm X offers similar insight into how an intelligent person can fall to the illusion of autonomy. Following a horrendous upbringing—his father lost his legs in an accident and died, and his mother was incarcerated in a mental asylum, leaving Malcolm to be raised in foster homes—Malcolm drifted into a life of crime. At age twenty he was arrested and convicted of theft. Since this was his first conviction, it should have carried a two-year sentence. Instead, Malcolm was sentenced to ten years in jail, a grotesquely disproportionate punishment. In prison Malcolm was recruited into the Nation of Islam, whose perspective on the world fitted Malcolm's experience perfectly. The white man really had dished him devilish treatment at just about every stage of his life. So when Elijah Mohammed, leader of the NOI, proclaimed that the white man really and truly was not just evil, but the devil incarnate, Malcolm bought into the whole doctrine—and then went on to spread that message with great panache and effectiveness, both in and out of prison, over the next twelve years. At that point, a visit to Mecca opened his eyes to the fact that the essential difference between blacks and whites is merely a matter of pigment. "I no longer subscribe to racism," he subsequently noted to a reporter. "I have adjusted my thinking to the point where I believe that whites are human beings—as long as this is borne out by their humane attitude toward Negroes." More to the point, however—or to the point we're making—Malcolm expressed bitter resentment that his immersion within the NOI blinded him to reality for so long. "I did many things then that I'm sorry for now. I was a zombie then . . . I was hypnotized, pointed in a direction and told to march. Well, I guess a man's entitled to make a fool of himself if he's ready to pay the cost. It cost me twelve years."

A zombie—that's what the man said. A zombie is a walking corpse that functions without thinking, imprisoned in a trance, its actions dictated by forces that it does not understand.

The moral, of course, is that we cannot become free until we begin to waken to the realization that we are imprisoned. But, because we *seem* to be in charge of our lives, we make the mistake of thinking that we *are* in charge of our lives. Thus the illusion of autonomy prevents us from acting to bring the zombie back to life.

Even now, you still probably can't really believe that *you* may be the victim of such an illusion. "Look," you say, "I can do anything I want, damn it! I am free to quit my job, if I want to. I can go hang-gliding, if I want to. I can burn this book, if I want to."

Like it or not, the hard fact is that you will only "want" to follow your programming. If you have been programmed to pursue risky endeavors, then you might indeed take up hang-gliding. But if your contract tells you to live carefully, then you will almost certainly never "want" to engage in such an activity, nor "want" to quit your job—even though you may believe that you could "if you really wanted to."

The illusion of autonomy is well illustrated by the behavior of a man whose brain was stimulated by an electrode during an operation. The stimulated area was the one controlling the right arm and the man raised that arm. When the operator asked him why he did so, he replied: "Because I wanted to."

This is the way the majority of lives are lived. Our programming sits like a bank of electrodes in our heads and governs our so-called thinking. We *think* we're making our own choices but in fact we're mostly following our innate desires and instincts. A lovely example of how even intelligent, sophisticated people rationalize the decision to follow their basest instincts lies in the words of Woody Allen, at the time of his "falling in love" with—and taking full-frontal nude photos of—the underage adopted daughter of Mia Farrow, Mr. Allen's steady companion. "The heart wants what it wants," said Mr. Allen to *Time* magazine. Ah, yes, of course—the *heart*.

Why the Illusion of Autonomy Is So Difficult to Dispel

> *How amusing it is to see the fixed mosaic of one's*
> *little destiny being filled out by tiny blocks of events—*
> *the enchantment of minute consequences with the*
> *illusion of choice weathering it all.*
>
> —Alice James

Spotting the illusion of autonomy at work in our everyday lives is no simple matter—and admitting to it is typically impossible. There are good reasons for this:

1. We have been programmed to believe that we are "free." From infancy on, we Westerners are constantly persuaded that adults are free to do whatever they want. And in America at least, a whole industry, the "success" industry, propagates the gospel that the world is our oyster—that we can do or get or be absolutely anything we want, just so long as we want it badly enough and will work hard enough. As a result, our psychic computer cards are riddled with punch marks that convince us, beyond any shadow of a doubt, that we are free to do our own thing.

In the West, we are also programmed to think "logically," and as long as we reject the notion that we're *really* driven by forces that we don't understand—which is how most prisoners and executives feel—then the brain automatically rejects the notion that our vaunted autonomy and logic is often merely an illusion—*without ever truly contemplating the idea.*

2. We are free to select the methods by which we pursue our scripts. We follow our programming in important matters, but by choosing time and place, we maintain the illusion that we are making our decisions freely, and that our behavior therefore is the result of free will. Consider, for example, the Atlanta broadcaster who, during a radio interview with me, queried the validity of the psychic contract concept, explaining proudly that he was a self-made man whose achievements were all his own and totally unrelated to any so-called psychic pact with his parents. Seeking to avoid a possibly fruitless argument, I asked him a question: "What did your father do?"

"Oh, nothing like me," he replied. "He was a Baptist preacher."

"But aren't you, too?" I asked. "Aren't you just commanding the airwaves to preach your own gospel to a much larger audience?" He paused. "So I am," he replied. "So I am. And, do you know, I run a talk-back show on Sundays and, over the years, nothing has given me more pleasure than when people have called to tell me that they *stayed home from church to hear my show.*"

Eric Berne recognized the phenomenon, and summarized it thus: "'Be devoted to your leader,' says the Nazi father, and the son devotes himself either to his Fascist leader, or to his leader in Christianity or to communism, with equal fervor. The clergyman saves souls in his Sunday sermons, and his daughter sallies forth to save them singing folk songs with her guitar. The father is a street sweeper and the son becomes a medical parasitologist, each in his own way cleaning up the offal that causes disease. The daughter of the good-natured prostitute grows up to be a nurse and comforts the afflicted in a more sanitary way."

Or take the case of Dick Green, a lawyer who took up ocean racing.

He was a totally inexperienced sailor, who, as he explained it, "just happened to hear the calling of the sea." In fact, that "calling" made him physically sick and terrified him. But he persisted, worked like a galley slave (his description), risked his life, and ultimately won many prizes.

Much later, when asked why he had felt compelled to embark upon such a course, he reached into his unconscious and found out. His father, he recalled, had always been a superb all-round sportsman, and a compulsive winner who would use any method to beat anyone, even his own son, Dick. But there was one thing that Dick's father could not do: he could not step on a yacht without experiencing nausea.

So, to become a "winner," just like his Dad, Dick "chose" a sport that enabled him to beat the "father in his head." However, when you look closely, you see that Dick sailed not to win, but to get even—a pursuit in which he felt compelled to risk his life.

Carl Jung observed that "nothing has a stronger influence on children than the unlived lives of their parents." Time and time again, the images of childhood overtake our lives in the most literal of ways.

3. We mistake rebellion for freedom. Many in my Rikers class mistake rebellion for freedom. As we've seen, however, rebellion is often just another way of dealing with a shaky sense of self-esteem and what seems to us to be an unattainable prime parental directive. We try to make ourselves feel better by turning our programming inside out, then doing the exact opposite of what we were told.

This syndrome is never more apparent than in the cases of teenagers who "discover themselves"—and get even—by becoming, for a time anyway, polar opposites of their parents. Children of the clergy become atheists, the industrialist's son discovers communism, and so it goes. Unfortunately, whenever we become knee-jerk rebels—rebels without a real cause—we remain confined in a mental prison. We fail to appreciate that we are merely reacting instead of making rational, autonomous choices.

4. We mistake unused programming for a new life. Responding to previously unused programming is a variant of "rebellion." That's why some middle-aged men—and, increasingly, women—suddenly change hairstyles, lifestyles, work styles, and companion styles.

In fact, unused programming, like the scripts of rebellion, are usually established during infancy, with specific instructions as to when they should be activated: for example, "When you are eighteen (or thirty or forty), use this new programming, or turn the old programming cards inside out."

Sometimes a person's programming reads: "When you are eighteen (or thirty or forty), delete all the programming in Series A and leave a vacuum." This vacuum must then be filled by a guru, a revolutionary leader, or a religion—any person or group with a new set of programs compatible with an automaton designed to follow orders.

Our programming may also specify when we shall stop functioning altogether. Consider, for example, the words of Mark Twain:

"I came in with Halley's comet in 1835. It is coming again next year, and I expect to go out with it. It will be the greatest disappointment of my life if I don't go out with Halley's comet. The Almighty has said, no doubt: 'Now here are these unaccountable freaks; they came in together, they must go out together.'"

Mark Twain's birth did, indeed, coincide with the perihelion of Halley's comet in November of 1835, and so did his death on April 21, 1910. But if there is a God, one would have to imagine that he's too busy to be organizing grandstand exits, even for such illustrious grandstanders as Mr. Twain. No, the truth, more likely, is that the simultaneous arrival of Twain and the comet became such an attention-getter for the infant that his mind became engraved with the need to achieve a final "coincidence." So, even though Twain predicted his destiny, he probably didn't realize that he had actually been programmed to seek it. If only he'd become aware of his "programming," he might have lived to be a hundred.

The illusion of autonomy denies us the capacity to break free from our prisons. Unfortunately, an automatic rejection of the concept of the illusion of autonomy further conceals our programming and keeps us thinking in the same old ways, resorting to the old obsolete grappling styles—and incarcerated in the same old prisons.

The people closest to us are usually very well aware of our blind spots—and keen to help us see the errors of our ways. You might think they could dispel the illusion of autonomy for us—and breathe some life into the zombie—simply by "having a few well-chosen words with us," thereby awakening us to our unconscious faults and foibles, but that's not so easy either. Let's see why.

WHY WE SHUN THE KEY THAT CAN UNLOCK OUR PRISON DOOR

Scotland's most illustrious poet, Robert Burns, memorably exclaimed, "Oh, would some God give us the gift to see ourselves as others see us!" A corporate client is hoping that I might just be able to impart that gift to one of its key executives, Tyrannical Ted. Ted looked quite brilliant in a rising market, but it topped out and his performance turned hopeless. His know-it-all attitude got worse instead of better, and his blame-shifting, butt-kicking style became even more marked. The problem is clear: Ted is rattling around inside a mental and emotional prison. His hold on his own sense of self-esteem has taken a beating— and he's reacting by trying to make himself *feel* better, but not addressing his *situation*. The corporation is hoping that I'll come up with the magic words to permit Ted to see the error of his pontificating, ears-closed ways—and then go on to change his behavior. Ted doesn't know it, but if I can't help him effect an immediate and dramatic change of attitude, he'll be fired within the week.

Consider another scenario, this time from my Rikers class. Fifty-year-old Robert has a question. "Why is it that we so quickly and accurately recognize other people's faults," he asks, "yet are incredibly slow to identify or acknowledge our own?" The query is prompted by the whining of a fellow classmate, formerly an investment banker, concerning his third conviction and subsequent incarceration for drunk driving. The inquiry is both deceptively simple and elegantly ironic, for Robert himself is a chronic offender—for drug use and domestic violence—who remains blind to his own destructive pattern. He's also nobody's fool, however, and he's waiting for a cogent answer. So let me take a crack at it.

The beginning of the problem is that we each project a mask to the world. This facade is intended to hide our insecurities, conceal our antagonisms, and promote acceptance by others. Common business facades include that of the charismatic leader, the dedicated, loyal follower, the star salesperson, and the corporate sage. In thinking about these facades it is useful to reflect upon tactics in a game of poker. The player with a poor hand seeks to bluff his opponent into believing that he has a great hand, whereas the player with a great hand stands to win most by conveying the impression he's holding only mediocre cards.

So, too, in the game of life. It is typically the insecure person who most wants to convince us that he's really a tough guy, and the strong, secure, savvy executive who feels no particular need to impress at all. That's why our old friend Baxter Barrow's priggish and defensive behavior contrasted so sharply with the confident candor of his no-nonsense chief executive.

As you see, we project the face that we believe is ours, hope is ours, and wish was ours; the persona that best suits our personality, weaknesses, stage in life, and immediate needs. The poet T.S. Eliot had J. Alfred Prufrock say, "I will prepare a face to meet the faces that I meet." Sure, but the various tremors that shape a particular mask—"the shocks that flesh is heir to," as Hamlet says—ultimately register, slowly, subliminally, and remorselessly, until we finally each possess the countenance we deserve. For some people this means that as the years advance they come closer to proffering an authentic self. For others, it means looking more and more like empty shells.

The Delphic Oracle famously counseled to Know Thyself. In fact, without the aid of a mirror we cannot actually observe our own behaviors, and the mind routinely hides our inner weaknesses from just about every attempted inward gaze. The mind achieves this goal of hiding our true selves from our own peeping eyes by means of Byzantine processes of which we remain blissfully—an apt word—unaware, *unconscious*, as Dr. Freud famously observed. The mind takes over the role of presenting and maintaining the facade. Not only does it concoct a persona to mask our weaknesses, it also has us dedicating our intellectual skills to the justification of our contradictory, overcompensatory behaviors while simultaneously denying their true roots.

WHY HYPOCRISY IS NORMAL

Ambrose Bierce defines a hypocrite as "a person who, professing virtues that he does not respect, secures the advantage of seeming to be what he despises." Hypocrisy might also merely refer to a consistent gap between beliefs and actions. Seeking to shine a light on such a lapse in our behavior is indeed difficult, since the mind routinely blocks that kind of insight. Sighting hypocrisies, faults, and foibles in others is much easier. Getting a person to acknowledge them, however, is a tricky and all too frequently futile exercise. The capacity of the failing executive to come up with excuses, alibis, and finger-pointings to rationalize personal nonperformance is almost breathtaking. One is left with the feeling that the fellow might actually believe his own lies.

There's a good reason for this, of course: he usually does. If we persist in trying to show him that his rationalizations are false, then he may regress to what I call the uproar syndrome. Now he's much more than defensive, he's angry, too—so here comes that flight of the bumblebee. He goes on the attack, points the parental digit, provokes a raucous argument, fails to let his would-be interrogator express or complete a pertinent criticism, threatens or resorts to fisticuffs—and then stalks off in a huff. In fact, his mind is protecting his persona. It sees the interrogator as akin to a misguided quack seeking to remove a bandage from a wound. If the fellow had to admit that he was actually wrong, he might lose his ability to function and suffer some kind of breakdown. This is why counseling sessions, performance appraisals, and termination interviews are best handled with sparse and very tactful words. It also accounts for the popularity of 360-degree survey offering objective, scientific "feedback" (not my favorite word) on how an executive is perceived by subordinates, peers, and superiors. This is usually an infinitely more palatable process than being berated by an angry boss. The subject of the survey can continue to rationalize that he's okay but that his presentation is not doing him justice. So he'll merely need to work at altering other people's faulty perceptions by adjusting appearances. In the process of so doing, of course, he begins to work upon his actual behaviors. And when he does this he gradually reduces the width of the gap between persona and performance and becomes a better person. Or so one hopes.

WHY WE DETEST PEOPLE WHO POSSESS OUR FOIBLES

A further paradox lies in our need to release the tension that builds as a result of concealing our deficiencies. The mind handles this problem very elegantly. It permits us to clearly sight our faults and foibles, but only in the behavior of other people. So listen closely to a preacher's sermon. The sin that provokes his fiercest denunciation is most likely to be his own.

Shakespeare's sonnet number 121—which could have been written by President Bill Clinton and dedicated to his various detractors at the height of the so-called Monica Lewinsky scandal—succinctly details this intriguing process. Consider the opening lines:

'Tis better to be vile than vile esteemed
When not to be receives reproach of being,
And the just pleasure lost which is so deemed,
Not by our feeling, but by others' seeing.

The poet is saying that if he is going to be accused of being a sinner, then he might as well be one, even though his accusers—whose spying eyes are spoiling all the pleasure—probably think he's having more fun than he actually is. The poet goes on to note, "they that level at my abuses reckon up their own"—in other words, my accusers are merely pruriently projecting their own unacknowledged lusty sins—of both the flesh and the mind—on to me. The final line expresses the poet's own overall judgment on the souls of those elected to govern us: "All men are bad, and in their badness reign."

It may be, of course, that this sonnet merely presents a sophisticated rationalization for doing the wrong thing, in which case the poet is deluding himself. But there's a price to be paid for such self-delusion, says Scott Peck, author of *The People of the Lie*. He asserts that the inability to face the truth ultimately leads a person to become evil—by which he means, I gather, to fall into the clutches of the devil. The kicker here is that such a person becomes blind to what has happened to him. This, according to Peck's theory, would be the fate of an unrepentant O.J. Simpson or even an unreconstructed Bill Clinton.

Bear in mind that even the most brilliant and sensitive people fall victim to the illusion of autonomy. One last example will serve to drive that point home—and point up a couple of other morals, too.

The Case of the Imprisoned Genius

Misfortunes one can reduce,
they come from the outside, they are accidents.
But to suffer for one's own faults
—ah—there is the sting of life.
—Oscar Wilde

"Give that to Oscar Wilde," said the Marquis of Queensberry, handing his visiting card to the hall porter at London's exclusive Albemarle Club, at 4:30 P.M. on February 18, 1895.

The card bore a handwritten message: to "Oscar Wilde posing as a Somdomite [sic]." Wilde might have corrected the spelling and returned the card. He might have laughed and tossed it away. A tortured bore whose angry visage inspired hilarity, the marquis was seldom taken seriously—Wilde had dubbed him the "screaming scarlet marquis." And the message was harmless: *posing* as a sodomite was an innocuous charge, surely, to make of a fellow who wore velvet suits and green carnations in 1895.

But Wilde chose to sue the marquis for defamation. In consequence, he set an epic tragedy into motion.

Lord Queensberry found and paid male prostitutes prepared to testify that Wilde was a practicing homosexual. The ring of truth hung in their tales. On the third day of the trial, when Wilde's barrister realized these tales were to be aired in court, he advised Wilde to drop the case, for if it went on to the end and the jury found the accusations true, the judge would order Wilde's arrest.

The lawyers guessed that even the withdrawal of Wilde's action might be construed as an admission of his homosexuality, and also lead to his arrest, so they told Wilde he would not be required in court on the final day, during which his lawyers would keep the case going so that Wilde could leave England. But, despite the forewarning, Wilde refused to flee. Why? This was Oscar's explanation: "Everyone wants me to go abroad. I have just been abroad, and now I have come home again. One can't keep going abroad, unless one is a missionary, or, what comes to the same thing, a commercial traveler."

His biographer Hesketh Pearson is less amusing, but very much to the point: "Despite the pleadings of all his friends, Wilde remained. Having little sense of reality, he could not imagine what was in store for him, and, if partially paralyzed by the shock, *he was half-hypnotized by the picture of himself as one predestined to suffer.*"

The rest is history. Wilde was arrested and tried, twice, for the "crime" of homosexuality. The first trial failed to produce a verdict. The second did. Wilde was found guilty and given the maximum sentence—two years with hard labor. The cruel treatment he received in prison ultimately killed him. Despite all of his former wealth, England's most popular playwright after Shakespeare died of cerebral meningitis some thirty months after his release, penniless, in disgrace, and exile in Paris, at age forty-six.

Perhaps, in some ways, Wilde never really left prison. Perhaps his own remark in conversation betrays the truth. "When I was a boy," he said, "my two favorite characters were Lucien de Rubempre and Julien Sorel. Lucien hanged himself, Julien died on the scaffold, and I died in prison."

Was Oscar Wilde "destined" to suffer this fate? Let's look at some of the facts and see what we make of them:

Oscar's father, William Wilde, was, like his father before him, a doctor. Though a grubby little man, William Wilde specialized in aural surgery, upon which subject he became the authority of the day. He wrote several travel books that gained him widespread fame, and he thus became a sought-after lecturer, a role he relished. Fame proved an aphrodisiac, and Dr. Wilde exploited its powers freely, for, despite his unwholesome appearance, he enjoyed a special taste for the ladies.

Neither his love of women nor the limelight extended, however, to the unfortunate events that surrounded the close of his career. Late in life he seduced an attractive eighteen-year-old patient and enjoyed a fairly long-standing affair with her. Then, when he tried to end the liaison, she sued him. Thus, Sir William Wilde (by then knighted for services to his patients) became the much-publicized defendant, and loser, of one of the most lurid court cases of his time.

Oscar Wilde's mother was a revolutionary, a poet, and a publicity seeker. She regarded herself as a genius. No one was inclined to argue with a woman of her pride, or her size.

She wanted a daughter but instead got Oscar. This fact so disappointed her that she dressed him as a girl "long after the age when the clothes of male and female children become distinctive." Oscar was pleased by his mother's strange habits. "I want to introduce you to my mother," he said to a college friend. "We have founded a society for the suppression of virtue."

He said many other intriguing things, of course, but two of his remarks are, for our purposes, of special interest. When asked his ambition in life, he replied: "God knows! I won't be a dried-up Oxford don, anyhow. I'll be a poet, a writer, a dramatist. Somehow or other I'll be famous, and if not famous I'll be notorious."

The other remark was made earlier, when he was still a mere boy and barely out of the frilly dresses his mother made for him: "I shall be famous," he said, "perhaps as an actor, or a dramatist. Or perhaps I will become the notorious defendant in a wicked court case."

It does not seem unreasonable to assume that William Wilde's trial had been imprinted on Oscar's psyche, and that he unconsciously—and perhaps sometimes consciously—sought to prove that he was as much a "man" as his father, by emulating him and becoming the tragic hero of his own psychodrama. Biographer Hesketh Pearson, who saw the entire tragedy, wrote that Oscar expected the harsh verdict "because in his fancy it had been preordained."

And *that*, dear reader, is what I've been doing my best to say from the start. That the whole tragedy was preordained. It was preordained *by* Wilde's fancy. He didn't just imagine his destiny—he *wrought* it.

Oscar Wilde became as rich, famous, and immoral as his illustrious father, and as quirky as his mother had programmed him to be. He also fulfilled his childhood dream: he became, as foretold, the notorious defendant in a wicked court case.

But did he get more than he bargained for? If Oscar had realized that unconscious forces were compelling him to destroy himself, would he still have "chosen" to sue the screaming scarlet marquis?

And what about you and me? If we knew, *for sure* that we were embarked upon similar misadventure, would we pass up the chance to waste our lives in prisons or undergo other purgatories of our making? I think that if Wilde had known what we now know he might have torn up that visiting card from the Marquis. But he did not know until too late, and he penned the following lamentation.

> *Strange I was not told*
> *the brain can hold*
> *in a tiny ivory cell*
> *God's Heaven and Hell*

The first point I am trying to make is that whether we live in heaven or in hell is entirely up to us. "Heaven, hell, the worlds are within us, man is the great abyss," said Amiel. "Do you not realize," asked Saint Paul, "that God's temple is within you?" Tentmaker Omar Khayyam put it this way:

> *I sent my Soul through the Invisible,*
> *Some letter of that After-life to spell:*

And by and by my Soul return'd to me,
And answer'd "I Myself am Heav'n and Hell:"

The second point I am trying to make is the importance of realizing that we do have a choice. Truly understanding that there are options is the only way to begin making heavens of our brief lives.

The kind of suffering that Oscar experienced is the clear sign of a very bad psychic contract. Paradoxically, however, such suffering also carries the seeds of enlightenment. Suffering, better than anything else, can raise our level of awareness, forcing us to question our own behavior, to wonder why we continually get ourselves into difficult situations, and to convince us that we must mend our ways. Under the spell of his programming, Oscar was witty and charming. In his prison cell he became truly wise and wrote, "At the beginning God made a world for each separate man, and in that world, which is within us, one should seek to live."

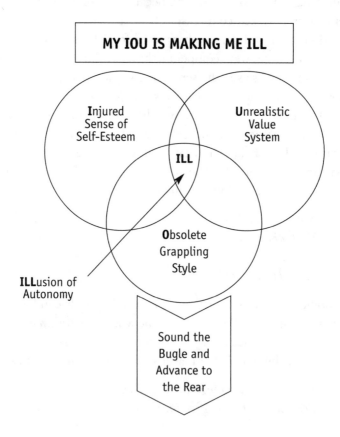

In a Nutshell

The challenge of life is to gain full possession of ourselves so that we can truly define our own successes and pursue our own best interests. Being able to do that, we are no longer imprisoned, and will never have to go back.

But how to do it?

Well, the very good news is that three trusty friends are ready, willing, able—and anxious—to help you transmute the three iron balls marked I and O and U into magic circles.

These three new buddies are on your side. They have your best interests at heart. They don't care how much energy they have to expend. They don't care whether they work nights or evenings. They're intending to be working around the clock, even when you're sleeping. I have to confess that their motives are not entirely altruistic, but the sad truth is that you'll never succeed in getting out of prison without their help. They work as a team, because each of them needs you to break out of prison for the same selfish reason. If you break out, then so will they.

So, turn the page, and let me introduce them, starting with the brainiest fellow first. His name is Cogitato.

PART TWO

RAISE COGITATO

& Begin to See the World with Open I's

Cogitato is the brains of the breakout team. Most inmates overlook his talents and relegate him to a funky sunken chamber and shackle him to prejudices, irrational beliefs, and wild-eyed conclusions—then wonder why he rebels and pits his skills against them.

Freedom seekers like to keep Cogitato in his favorite place, behind the eyes with a clear view of what's going on, between ears to catch every piece of advice that comes his way, and slightly above the nose to suss out the scent of baloney.

The keys to Cogitato's happiness are knowledge, reason, and innovation. He likes to read, and his favorite quote is from philosopher Henry Van Dyke, "No amount of energy will take the place of thought. A strenuous life with its eyes shut is a kind of insanity."

CHAPTER 6

How to Wake Up in Prison

& Transmute Those Iron Balls into Magic Circles

Awakening begins when a man realizes that he is going nowhere
and does not know where to go.
—Georges Gurdjieff

It's four in the morning and thirty-two-year-old Eddie is contemplating his choices. Yesterday he'd been a smooth-talking hustler of investor funds for a big-name Wall Street firm. The remuneration used to be great but recently hadn't been so hot. His employers came to assess him as the sufferer of two related sales diseases: burnout and call reluctance. At five o'clock last night they fired him. The termination is a blot on his copybook. The big money he pulled down surely won't come his way again. To make matters worse he recently married. Muffy, currently six months pregnant, had been looking forward to enjoying the sweet life. Sure, they have a million dollars in the bank. But they were just about to sink all of that into a very modest three-bedroom Park Avenue apartment. Now that he's unemployed no co-op board will approve him for such a purchase. How, after all, will he fund the monthly maintenance? And how will they now afford a nanny? Or ever send their child to adequate kindergartens and schools? And, really, what the hell is he going to do with the rest of his life?

Eddie doesn't know it, but if he went to the window of his luxury high-floor rental apartment and trained his telescope eastward in the direction of LaGuardia Airport he might just spot Rafael. Rafael is now thirty-seven years old and about to be released from Rikers Island jail. He's been incarcerated for eight months. He used to be a hustler. He did drugs and a lot of other bad things. A warden drops three bronze subway tokens into his empty palm. "Good luck," he says.

Rafael studies the tokens. They'll get him into the city. A friend has offered him a place to sleep for a week. He could also stay with his long-suffering mother. But with a criminal record and only rudimentary clerical skills, finding a job will be difficult indeed. Will he become one of the 80 percent of ex-cons who return to Rikers? He makes a vow to himself to create a life among the lucky 20 percent who manage to survive outside. Hey, he reasons, if I can pay the bills and stay within the law, survival will be enough.

Eddie has a million dollars, a loving wife, and a heavy heart. Rafael has neither money nor prospects, but a nice attitude and a good mind. Eddie and Rafael have a lot in common right now. Both are facing crucial choices. Both need Cogitato to shine a little light.

Sight the Light and Catch the Wizard

I really like the story about the man who asks a question of an incredibly self-possessed visitor.

"Are you a god?" he queries.

"No."

"Are you a sorcerer?"

"No."

"Are you a genius?"

"No."

"What are you then?"

"I am awake," says the Buddha.

To be truly awake is to see the world as it really is, to know one's place in it, to figure out one's best interests.

The specific event or insight that triggers an awakening varies from person to person. José, the feisty fellow who wanted to know about reality, began to awaken during our classroom discussion of Frank Baum's wonderful story of *The Wizard of Oz*.

You'll remember that the heroine, Dorothy, played by everybody's sister, Judy Garland, races over the rainbow along with her dog, Toto, in search of the enchanted Land of Oz and the wonderful wizard who lives there.

Dorothy is aided in her quest by a tin man who rusts in the rain, a noisy lion who beneath his brave front is terrified of the world, and a scarecrow who can't think straight. Dorothy's attempts to find the wizard are thwarted at nearly every turn by the wicked witch of the west.

At journey's end, however, Dorothy and Toto are ushered in to meet the wizard. His awesome visage appears on a giant screen; his voice booms from loudspeakers; smoke fills the air. Dorothy, very naturally, is frightened. She is not too frightened, however, to notice strange movements behind a curtain. Then, out of playful curiosity, Toto springs forward and tugs the curtain aside to reveal the wizard—and much less.

Dorothy discovers that, in fact, the wizard is no wizard at all— merely a wizened old man, furiously manipulating controls to magnify his voice, his image, and his assorted effects.

In this moment Dorothy realizes that she is dreaming, and she begins, in every sense of the word, to awaken. She realizes that she has been in pursuit of an imaginary world, and that the Land of Oz, and all its characters, exist only in her own head. This realization sets Dorothy free. She escapes from her dream and returns "home," where she rediscovers the wizard and the whole cast of characters. This time, however, she sees them as they really are. She finds that the wicked witch was merely the memory of an unpleasant schoolteacher. The lion, the tin man, and the scarecrow are the imperfect neighbors of everyday life. The wizard is a trickster from the local circus.

Dorothy's awakening brings an understanding of human frailty. It also evokes the realization that *these people comprise, in their way, all there is or ever will be to life*. She sees that it is better to live without illusions than to be chased through life by the ghosts of one's own unconscious. Armed with this knowledge, Dorothy sets off again on a greater adventure: to enjoy the world as it *is*, and not go dreaming about what may or may not be over the rainbow.

A tragic irony in this whole tale is that the moral of the story, so clear to Dorothy the fictional heroine, eluded Judy Garland the star. She committed the film script to heart and made "Over the Rainbow" an unforgettable song. She failed, however, to hear the message in her own lines. Judy Garland never adjusted to the real world and finally died following the administration of more tranquilizing drugs than her system could handle.

The causes of Judy Garland's tragedy might lie in an even deeper moral to the Oz story. The Land of Oz, as any Freudian might tell you, is the unconscious memory of childhood. The wizard is the all-powerful father figure that each of us projects onto an internal screen—and whose approval we seek. The wicked witch is someone standing between Dorothy and the wizard; probably a sister—or a mother—competing with Dorothy for her father's attention. And, of course, Toto, the dog, symbolizes Dorothy's own intuitive processes.

In this context then, Judy Garland never really grew up. She spent her entire "adult" life trapped in a nightmarish dream. Hollywood, for her, was not so much a place as a state of mind in which she was terrorized, and, finally, frightened to death by characters who, outside of her own head, did not exist.

The point is that even though we may think that we are fully awake, we remain in the Land of Oz until we realize that we are dreaming. To make that realization, we must somehow see behind the scenes and discover the true identities of the characters who inhabit the land of our unconscious. Only when we permit ourselves to discover the identity of *our* particular wizard, do we begin to awaken. The realization of having been spellbound by such a figure is usually the key element in *any* awakening.

It was no accident, as I'm sure you realize, that José raised his fist on the word father, for his own father had been both cantankerous and abusive, and José had never overcome his resentment of that old man. In fact, he'd been ambivalently using him as a role model, and then striking out at just about any authority figure that happened to appear in his life. When José finally apprehended the reality behind his behavior, his illusion of autonomy began to dissolve.

If you harbor the widespread suspicion that the illusion of autonomy might apply to prison inmates, but would not hamper the typical hard-headed executive, then consider a parallel example from the corporate world.

BREAKING THE SPELL ON TERRY TRANCE

Terry Trance raised his hand in one of my seminars. "Your ideas about psychic contracts may apply to some people," he said, "but they certainly don't apply to me." To "prove" that he alone was in charge of his life, he related his life story. He punctuated the tale with these words:

"So you can see yourself that it is impossible for my father, or anyone else but me, to be in charge of my life."

Terry had explained that he and his father were not on speaking terms, and had not been for many years. The father, according to Terry, was a man with a "superiority complex, who always treated me like a know-nothing little boy."

Terry paid his own way through college, and earned a first-class degree. But this did not give him the "feeling" that he was "well educated." So, in midlife, he went back to college as a part-time student and completed two more degrees. After that he took up marathon running, at which he also excelled, driving himself unmercifully, ultimately ruining both of his knees.

It seemed a fair guess that Terry had devoted his life to an unconscious competition with his father, and I decided to test the thesis. "You certainly beat your father at being an intellectual," I said. The remark carried the presumption that a contest was in progress, and that Terry was winning. Despite the fact that Terry had denied both of those things, he now nodded his head in agreement.

"I've beaten him at being an intellectual," said Terry, raising his voice, "and I've beaten him at athletics. And I'm beating him in business, too." Now Terry's eyes were blazing. "And I'm going to go on beating him," he said, and his fist began to bang his desk, "and beating him, and beating him again!"

Suddenly Terry's illusion of autonomy was dispelled. He realized that he had really returned to college in order to prove that his arguments were as good as those of his father. He saw that he had really spent his life trying to catch his father's attention. Later, explaining why he had wanted to argue the matter, Terry explained that "I like to pick holes in people's arguments, because my father was always so cocksure of himself."

The story shows how difficult it can be to acknowledge the true roots of one's own behavior. Terry's immediate reaction to the notion of parental programming had been to deny that it applied to him. It's this knee-jerk rejection of the mental prison concept—and especially of the illusion of autonomy—that stops us from even *wanting* to find the key that will unlock the doors to freedom.

The Four A's in Awake

The illusion of autonomy is like a magic curtain whose existence is hidden until you decide that it *might* exist. It was not so much looking, but *wishing* to look that triggered Dorothy's awakening, for that decision represented a tentative refusal to accept that things were as they seemed. So make a conscious decision to contemplate the notion that you might not, in fact, be fully awake.

Breaking out of prison is akin to waking from a dream of Oz. *Only when you waken do you realize you were dreaming.*

Joseph Heller, in his novel *Something Happened,* has his protagonist, Bob Slocum, waking from such a sleep, and complaining that the illusion of autonomy has denied him the capacity to run his own life. "How did I get here?" he asks. Then he answers, "Somebody pushed me. Somebody set me off and clusters of other hands must have set themselves to the controls at various times, for I would not have picked this way for the world."

Eugene O'Neill, in the play *Long Day's Journey Into Night,* has the mother make a similar observation: "None of us can help the things life has done to us. They're done before you realize it, and once they're done they make you do other things until at last everything comes between you and what you'd like to be, and you have lost your true self forever."

But, how, if you think you are already awake, can you begin to comprehend that you are really asleep?

The first step out of this bind—and out of prison—is to effect a conscious change of *attitude.* All that is required is a decision to accept and examine the notion that we *might not* really be fully awake. By doing this we actually suspend the illusion of autonomy long enough hopefully, to achieve two things: first, to contemplate our state of consciousness, and, second, to trigger a change in it.

Deciding to suspend the illusion of autonomy is akin to Dorothy peeping behind the wizard's curtain. (Toto's actions merely symbolized Dorothy's own childlike wish to tug at the curtain.) And it was not so much looking, but *wishing* to look that triggered Dorothy's awakening, for that decision represented a tentative refusal to accept that things were as they seemed.

The illusion of autonomy is like a magic curtain whose existence is hidden until we decide that it *might* exist. So, even just *contemplating* the curtain's existence triggers the process that will eventually enable us to see the curtain and pull it aside.

Actually drawing the curtain will dispel the illusion of autonomy, and open our eyes to the realization that we have been living in a mental prison.

At that point, we will be *compelled* to acknowledge the existence of another level of consciousness, simply because there is no way around that recognition. At that point we can no longer base our actions upon the belief—the *illusion*—that a thing is true merely because we consciously believe that it is. Now, like it or not, we are pushed into a new *kind* of existence—a world without walls.

By my reckoning, then, there are four A's in *awake*, each of which elevates the plateau of consciousness:

➤ *Attitude:* Being prepared to contemplate the notion that an illusion of autonomy might lie at the heart of one's problems.

➤ *Analysis:* Examining one's life with a view to connecting up the dots.

➤ *Answers:* Spotting the faulty beliefs that underlie emotional distress, unhappy consequences, and mistakes.

➤ *Action:* Making real changes in life's problem areas.

Identifying and acknowledging previously unrecognized patterns of behavior inevitably triggers a change of consciousness. Eyes become opened to the realization of not making authentic, rational, conscious choices. At that point, one is compelled to acknowledge the existence of another level of consciousness simply because there is no way around that recognition. No longer can actions be based upon the belief—the illusion—that a thing is true merely because we consciously believe that it is. Now, like it or not, we are pushed into a new kind of existence—the kind of existence in which the following two parables suddenly make perfect sense.

A fisherman was rowing his boat upstream on a foggy morning. Suddenly, another vessel appeared out of the mist and came surging downstream toward him. "Be careful! Be careful!" he shouted. Instead of changing course, however, the other boat gradually picked up speed then came crashing into him, almost sinking his own fragile craft. The fisherman became enraged and began to shout and curse the other person. Upon looking more closely, however, he realized that there was no one in the other boat.

Instead of recognizing the challenge at hand, the fisherman made a foolish assumption that led to an unhappy outcome. And then, compounding the error, he tried to shift the blame to "the other person." With any good luck, the needless mishap may have taught the fisherman the first lesson of enlightenment: *that we must always assume responsibility for the voyage of our own lives.* As children we have a right to be looked after and protected from misfortune, but as enlightened adults we must stop leaning on others and instinctively look out for our own best interests. The short lesson, then, is that as adults we are *on our own.*

Which leads to the second story.

A sojourner visited heaven and hell. In both places people were seated at a round table upon which many delectable foods were arrayed. Chopsticks a yard long were tied to the diners' right hands, and their left hands were strapped to their chairs. In hell, no matter how they stretched their arms the chopsticks were too long for them to insert food into their mouths. They grew impatient, got their hands and chopsticks tangled with one another, and sent the delicacies flying all over the place. In heaven, however, the diners cheerfully used the long chopsticks to pick out someone else's favorite food and feed it to him, and in turn were fed by others—and all enjoyed their meal in harmony.

The second lesson of enlightenment, then, is that inane rivalry and "looking out for number one" create a hell, and the acceptance of interdependence creates a heaven. How do we resolve the apparent contradiction presented by the first two lessons of enlightenment? The answer is simple. The enlightened person realizes that *the most effective way to fend for oneself is to make a conscious contribution to others.* A two-way process is involved. We cannot merely sit at the table of life and expect to be fed. That may work for a while, but usually not very well, and ultimately not at all. If, on the other hand—pun intended—we provide a service that contributes to the well-being of others, then that contribution will return to us as if by some divine force.

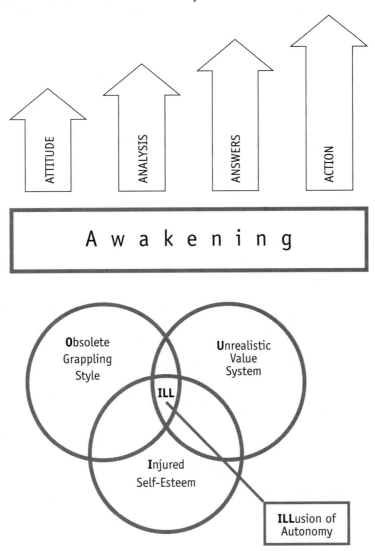

CHAPTER 7

MAGIC CIRCLE NUMBER 1

The Integrated Value System
How It Transforms Mistakes into Virtues & Challenges into Savvy Choices

He wagged his finger, stamped his foot, and shook his surly head.
"I'll never make the same mistake again," he firmly said,
Then he strutted back into the world and made
A new mistake instead.

—Chandler Haste

"I've made so many mistakes," sighed Alberto. "If only I could begin life again."

I should perhaps weep but instead I smile. "You're only twenty years old, Alberto. Your life has just begun."

"*That's* the point. Already I'm a criminal and there's no way to overcome my horrible history."

Should I confide to Alberto that I've sometimes dreamed of having two lives? In the first I'd make the mistakes that seem compulsory, then in the second, I'd get rich off them. No, don't tell him that.

"The longer I live, Alberto, the more I think that the blunders we're not allowed to make in our youth demand to be made at greater cost and less benefit later in life."

"So what's the moral?"

"That it's better to make a mistake in the beginning than in the end. Isadora Duncan said that if she had her life to live over she'd make the same mistakes, only sooner."

"Isadora who?"

"She was a flamboyant dancer who wore a long scarf and rode in a topless sports car—or did, until the day the tail of the scarf wrapped itself around the back wheel and strangled her. It was the one mistake she never recovered from."

"I'm a criminal not a dancer."

"We're all criminals, Alberto. It's a matter of degree. Crime is as human as charity."

"So it's okay to be a criminal?"

"Sometimes it's necessary. The writer Joseph Conrad said that the real significance of crime is in its being a breach of faith with the community. He felt that crime makes things worse for everyone, not just the criminal, and might actually be a sin."

"What's a sin?"

"Something very human and excusable."

"Like a mistake?"

"Yes, a mistake—a choice that leads to an unhappy outcome, something we didn't really want."

"Like getting arrested?"

"I think so."

"You only *think* so?"

"Here's the point, Alberto. Mistakes are lessons in disguise. But sometimes the disguises are so good that we fail to recognize either the mistake or the lesson. If we spot our mistakes, however, then we really can learn some very worthwhile things."

"Like what?"

"Like how not to hurt ourselves and others by making the same mistake again."

"I wish someone would teach me that."

"People have tried, I'm sure. The trouble is that we only pay attention to the things we discover for ourselves."

"So give me the crash course. Tell me what I need to discover."

"Well, I guess the first thing to remember is that it is important to make mistakes. That's the way we grow. It's the people who do nothing that make the biggest mistake. Their entire lives become mistakes. George Bernard Shaw, who wrote some clever plays, went even further. He said that a life spent making mistakes is more useful and more honorable than a life wasted doing nothing. And remember this, the fellow who never makes a mistake generally takes his orders from someone who does. Now, second, and this applies to you, especially, Alberto, we make mistakes because we have no other option."

"Absolutely none?"

"None that we're fully aware of. We merely choose the best from a set of limited options."

"Who sets the limit?"

"Family, friends, society at large—and ourselves. If we don't believe in our own abilities then we automatically exclude countless possibilities."

"So there's a problem in believing the wrong things?"

"Mistaken beliefs get us into trouble at every turn."

"Is there a list of those that I can bone up on?"

"I'm putting one together. I'll give it to you later."

"Maybe that'll help. What else should I know?"

"That we all need to be able to think logically. I'll give you a list of misleading notions that keep tripping people up."

"What's the most important thing for me to learn, right now?"

"Not to try to shift the blame to others for your mistakes. A mistake we don't accept is like a letter that hasn't been delivered. We make yet another mistake when we refuse to admit our mistakes. We can't learn from what we pretend never happened. We have to be honest and accept our mistakes in order to grow. If we don't learn from them, we repeat them until we do."

"I guess we should never repeat a stupid mistake."

"That is a very big should. The truth is, being human, we're more likely to repeat a mistake than to profit from it. But stupidity is the name we give to other people's mistakes. We usually chalk up our own to experience—which has been defined as the realization that you just made the same mistake again."

"So what's the use of experience, then?"

"Ultimately, we incorporate the lessons it teaches into our behavior. If you continually board the wrong train there's no use running down the corridor in the other direction. Someday we have to learn to get onto the right train."

"How do I find the right train?"

"I've got four rules for you, so listen up."

1. Respect Logic

Reason is developed by going against habit and repetition,
by following a legitimate whim; but not doing as others do.
—*A.R. Orage*

We act according to value judgments because it is impossible to know everything. What we can do, however, is rid ourselves of wild-eyed beliefs, wishful thinking, hopeless diffidence, and mindless certitude by replacing irrational beliefs with facts or reasonable assumptions, and negative, irrational thoughts with positive, rational ones. The good news is that since our emotional experience is the result of our cognitive processes, when we restructure our thinking our feelings eventually follow suit.

We cannot behave rationally, however, until we learn to think clearly. This requires freeing oneself from internal and external demons by being able to examine a situation rationally, then choosing our own true best interests. This is easy to say, less easy to do. Encouragement to keep trying may lie in the fact that it is *impossible* to make rational choices until we realize how we are manipulated by our own unconscious.

One of the reasons that Berry, from my Rikers class, gave for refusing to affirm the debate proposition, "God does not exist," was that he believed he had absolute firsthand proof of God's actual existence. "I was making a drug deal," he explained. "Somebody from another gang stepped up and fired three bullets into our group. One man died, two were wounded, only three of us weren't hit. No bullet touched me. It was a miracle. God spared me."

"But there's another way to analyze that situation, Berry," I replied. "Three bullets were fired at six people, so unless one bullet were to inflict a multiple injury, then at least three persons were always going to walk away unharmed. So maybe you just happened to be one of those people. But, anyway, if there really is a God, why did he let anyone get hit?"

Berry merely blinked. Like most prison inmates, he regards God as the force that rescued him from the streets and brought him to the relative safety of jail. To Berry's way of thinking, God is akin to an omnipotent parent, hovering in the background watching over a hapless infant. I didn't want to mess with Berry's God, but I did need him to realize that he was discounting the force of his own actions. I needed him to acknowledge that the divinity responsible for Berry's incarceration was none other than himself. And that it was within his own power to turn his life around, too.

I've seen a similar syndrome at work with corporate inmates. They, however, assign omnipotent powers to the corporation rather than God. Belonging to an esteemed and powerful organization confers status along with a steady income. On the downside, however, they feel like hapless victims within an awesome structure, especially when younger colleagues so often win fast-track promotions over them. Ultimately, the supposedly loyal, long-serving employees come to hate the company, yet are afraid to quit because it would entail a loss of identity as well as the need to fend for themselves in a threatening world. Such individuals find it difficult—or even impossible—to think clearly about their predicaments. The unconscious remains in charge, and intellect is used to deny that fact, and rationalize the failure to pursue freedom outside the corporate cage.

A short course in logic, diligently pursued, can be the beginning of intellectual independence, especially if followed by the systematic acquisition of knowledge—not knowledge of beliefs, mind you, but of facts. Armed with logic and enough facts, we can apply what we have learned and start thinking for ourselves. This will probably entail not being quite so sure of one's opinions, but that could in itself represent a giant step in the right direction. So let's look at some of the most common errors of logic.

- ► **All-or-nothing lumping.** Oversimplifying an issue and then presenting too narrow a range of possibilities. "Either you are for capital punishment and against criminality, or you are opposed to capital punishment and in favor of criminality—it's just as simple as that!" Hey, you've restricted the available options to merely two and presented a *false dilemma*. You're trying to force a choice between two unpalatable options. The issues are infinitely more complex. A lot of intelligent people are opposed to criminal behavior, for example, yet revolted by the notion of the death penalty.

➤ **Question begging.** "The question is whether we can release this prisoner when he shows absolutely no capacity to fit back into society." The real issue is *not* whether we release the prisoner. The real issue is whether the prisoner has learned enough to become a decent citizen. The speaker has avoided having to prove the real allegation by assuming it to be a fact—thereby leading whoever listens to him to make the same assumption.

➤ **Statistic dumping.** Statistics can be true without telling the whole story. "Four out of five doctors recommend the XYZ painkiller." True enough, maybe, but the survey was of only five doctors, four of whom were on the XYZ payroll!

➤ **Conclusion jumping.** Some people get all their exercise by jumping to conclusions. The Romans had a term for the most infamous conclusion-jumping fallacy. They called it *post hoc ergo propter hoc*, which, in plain English means, "after this, therefore because of this." The fallacy lies in confusing *after* with *because*. "Local crime immediately increased when this man was paroled from jail—he is clearly to blame." Just because crime increased when the parolee was released does not mean that he personally committed the crimes. The conclusion simply does not follow from the premise.

➤ **Backward stumping.** Reasoning backwards is the staple fallacy of stereotyping. "All politicians are liars. This man is a politician—and therefore a liar." Not at all. The first statement is too broad to justify the conclusion.

➤ **False-analogy trumping.** Misleading comparisons that don't hold up because the items being compared are insufficiently alike. "A criminal is like a poisonous snake. He'll always come back and bite you." Hey, what about the ex-offenders who go on to live productive lives? Or people whose so-called crimes weren't really crimes at all—Gandhi, for example?

➤ **Guru plumping and Bible thumping.** Appealing to authority is a common debating ploy. Just because the Roman Catholic Church has declared the Pope's decrees infallible does not mean that he is infallible. Just because something intelligent appears in an ancient holy writ, this does not mean that it is true. One could more easily make the opposite argument; the holy writ is probably obsolete precisely because it is ancient. The Newtonian law, "what goes up must come down," for example, became obsolete the day the Sputnik was launched—and was therefore *never* a law at all. Oh, sure, Newton *said* that it was, but, alas, like so many apparent experts, he got it wrong. Better to rely upon logic than upon vaunted gurus and gods.

➤ **Compro clumping.** To compro clump is to seek to impose a compromise solution on all parties. Reasonable humans reflexively tend to go along with compro clumping. What we need to realize, however, is that if you say two-plus-two makes four, and I say two-plus-two makes six—that any compromise we agree upon, say that two-plus-two equals five, is going to be flat out wrong, and therefore cause a long-term problem.

2. Respect Confusion

> *The struggle for knowledge has a pleasure in it,*
> *something like wrestling with a fine woman.*
> —Lord Halifax

There are many ways to see the world. We can choose to see it through the eyes of a prophet—such as Buddha, Christ, or Mohammed. Or we can see it through a psychologist's eyes—Freud, Jung, Adler, or Skinner. Or we might prefer to perceive it through the scientific prism of an Isaac Newton or an Albert Einstein. In fact, the best way to see the world is *through our own eyes.* But to achieve this, we must first understand what the great minds through history have had to offer, for any philosophy is a product of the time, the problems, the whole orientation of the person who promulgated it—*and may therefore be totally inapplicable to our current situation.*

At Rikers I present a brief course in great ideas. We look at the key concepts that have shaped civilization. Social issues like justice, democracy, and freedom. Personal issues such as free will, destiny, self-understanding. Some people in authority have been shocked that prison inmates even understand these ideas, let alone respond to them. But I do know this: truly profound ideas are immediately appealing and *easy* to grasp. Sometimes they come clothed in language that obscures their simple beauty, but that can be remedied. It is the corporate inmate who responds less quickly to a great idea—say the notion of justice—than a prison inmate. The concept seems a little remote for the corporate inmate, whereas it is of intrinsic interest to the prison inmate. There's no need to complete a degree in philosophy to get a handle on these ideas. Many short courses are available. There is also an increasing number of *very* accessible books available, some even in a cartoon format.

Self-knowledge is a key component of all knowledge. We're always changing; it's very difficult for us to predict what the future holds in terms of future growth. It may indeed be foolish even to try to do so. What we can do, if we're open-minded enough, is discover how we got to be the way we are. And, again, for an open-minded person—or a person who has become open-minded—discovering the hitherto hidden forces at work in one's life it can be surprisingly *easy*.

The beauty of gaining knowledge is that we also learn humility. We find that the world is not as simple as any one guru tries to make it seem. Knowledge brings doubts and exceptions and limitations. Ultimately we are forced to think for ourselves. Now the world is suddenly more complex. Yet it is simpler, too, for now we have learned the inescapable: that until we have learned enough to be confused we know nothing worth knowing.

Zealots and ideologues can typically only see the world through one prism. The prism of ultra-patriotism, for example, denies many American patriots the capacity to grasp the concept that flag burning is an expression of the freedom that the flag represents, and that to refuse to allow others to burn it in sincere symbolic protest is to diminish that freedom *and* the value of the flag.

The ultimate aim of what I call *constructive confusion* is clarity. This comes when we possess the capacity to view the world through several prisms, contemplate consciously the virtues of each, and then finally to either select—or create—a perspective that will actually work in the current situation. We might even create an entirely new perspective all of our own. An example is the French viewpoint on flag burning, which they choose to view as a private property issue. It is a therefore entirely within the law to burn a flag paid for with one's own personal funds, but a criminal offense to burn a flag that is public property.

3. Respect Intuition

The philosopher and poet Tagore said that a mind that is all logic is like a knife that is all blade and "makes the hand bleed that uses it." This may seem paradoxical, but the subconscious mind inevitably knows more than we consciously realize. It points the way in any logical inquiry: to respect intuition is merely to incorporate that rich source of information into the equation under consideration. Ralph Waldo Emerson, in his classic essay on self-reliance, referred to "the inner gleam" and wrote:

> A man should learn to watch that gleam of light, which flashes across his mind from within, more than the luster of the firmament of bards and sages. Yet he dismisses without notice his thought, because it is his. In every work of genius we recognize our own reflected thoughts; they come back to us with a certain alienated majesty. Great works of art have no more abiding lesson for us than this. They teach us to abide by our own spontaneous impression with good-natured inflexibility when the whole cry of voices is on the other side. Else tomorrow a stranger will say with masterly good sense precisely what we have thought and felt all the time, and we shall be forced to take with shame our own opinion from another.

The concept of an inner gleam is confirmed by recent research suggesting that certain cells make up a "survival mechanism" which, functioning independently of our conscious processes, monitors our behavior. This could also be the authentic "self," of which psychologist Dr. Abraham Maslow observed: "We have, each of us, an essential inner nature which is intrinsic or natural. The inner core is weak rather than strong. It is easily drowned out by learning, cultural expectations, fear, and disapproval. Authentic selfhood can be defined as being able to hear these impulse voices within oneself."

Proponents of "Inner Tennis," like those of Zen archery, are in agreement that, when we let "it" do the work, we survive in an almost miraculous fashion. Like all athletes, however, the Zen archer also agrees that conscious practice harnesses and hones this deeper inner force, so we must make the conscious effort in order to enhance the functioning of the inner gleam.

In essence then, we must abide by reason, until reason tells us to let go. Then we should let go completely and follow our intuition—which, incidentally, the dictionary defines as being "taught from within." Freud gave similar advice. He said we should attend to minor decisions consciously. In large matters where facts are unavailable, however, he distilled his advice to three words: "Follow your heart."

4. Despise and Dispel Imprisoning Beliefs

The Buddha's first three noble truths are that 1) suffering is the condition of mankind; 2) the cause of suffering is desire; and 3) to relieve our suffering we should remove its cause, which is to say that we should surrender our desires.

My own observation is that the cause of most suffering is not so much desire as it is infantile desire, by which I mean desire predicated upon infantile illusions.

Such desires and such illusions spring, in essence, from dependency, from an essentially infantile desire to retrieve the bliss of childhood, the warmth of the crib, or the security of the womb.

Similarly, the desire to find a substitute for the parent whose comforting head was sighted at the other end of the cradle causes some people to spend their lives seeking solace from sources outside themselves.

For most people, then, the pursuit of happiness means trying to gratify one of two wishes: 1) the wish to return to the preferred position of childhood; or 2) the wish to find a "higher head" in the form of someone to tell us how to live our lives.

In fact, the gratification of any infantile desire tends to leave us feeling empty rather than fulfilled. The first step to liberating oneself from these feelings is to discover the mistaken, imprisoning beliefs that underlie emotional pains and gird mental prisons. Let's look at some of the more common examples and consider how to dispel them.

THE NO. 1 INFANTILE ILLUSION

On the raw, cold sixth day of December 1791, a third-class burial service was held, and a young man's body consigned to a pauper's grave. Only the grave digger came to the burial. No tombstone or cross marked the grave. Now, no one knows where it was.

The lost grave harbors the dust of Wolfgang Amadeus Mozart. He was a genius from infancy, and his ability to play the harpsichord was declared divine. When the boy composed music, it seemed as if God were writing.

The divinity of this "radiant angel," as he was called, seemed confirmed by a feat he performed at Rome during Holy Week. Each year the *Misere* of Gregorio Allegri was performed by the papal choir. A papal decree forbade its performance anywhere else, and the only existing copy of the work was jealously guarded—any attempt to reproduce it was punishable by excommunication. Mozart heard the performance twice, then, in the privacy of his rooms, wrote down the entire complex contrapuntal score from memory. When the Pope heard of this incredible achievement he awarded the boy the cross of the Order of the Golden Spur.

And so the child became the musical wonder of the age, the favorite of the Viennese court, and the apple of the Austrian emperor's eye.

Unfortunately, as the angel became a young man, his mortality became increasingly apparent, and, in consequence, Mozart failed to retain the fascination of either the emperor or his court. Musicians of the day assumed that a person of Mozart's genius would be appointed court musician, but the elevation was long in coming. When it finally arrived, the emperor, like so many rich men who imagine themselves to be generous, more than lived up to his reputation for niggardliness. He slashed Mozart's miserable stipend by more than half, leaving him with less than a living wage.

Mozart became ill as well as poor, and to pay his way he did the only thing he knew: composed music. It continued to thrill the greatest minds of the age, but the general public, always fickle, lost interest in this all-too-perfect work. Mozart now composed letters to his friends in which he literally begged for money. He received little.

Penniless and by then critically ill, in a desperate attempt to earn the money to buy back his health, Mozart finally embarked upon a musical race with death. In the last months of his life he wrote his three greatest symphonies, a musical mass, and an opera.

That opera, *The Magic Flute*, was his last best hope, and, in fact, after a quiet debut, it became a great musical and finantial success. Pain-wracked and bedridden, Mozart would sometimes hold his watch and point out to his friends the exact moment when one of his favorite arias from this opera was being sung in the theater. The producer of the opera, however, cheated Mozart out of his royalties.

Mozart knew only thirty-five winters before he died, but his music is as vital as ever, and his place in the musical firmament seems assured. The tragedy is that he deserved so much more, and that he could have produced so much more. But no one of sufficient influence cared enough to try to save him.

All of which brings us, dear reader, to this vital question:

If no one saved Mozart, who will save *you?*

The answer, of course, is that no one will—we must save ourselves. Buddha saw this very clearly. "Work out your own salvation," he said. "Do not depend on others." Leaning too long upon a crutch is crippling. So, too, is leaning upon other people. Our faculties wither, and we become financial, intellectual, and emotional cripples, unable to pay, to think, or to fend for ourselves.

Emotional dependence was at the heart of Mozart's tragedy. As a child he was denied contact with harsh reality, and pampered without thought for his own ultimate well-being. "You are a little sorcerer," said the emperor to the long-haired boy in silk hose and a puff-sleeved velvet jacket. The little sorcerer lay, at that moment, in the arms of the empress, who fondled him as though he were a doll. Only Madame de Pompadour appeared aloof. When she turned her face away at his effort to kiss her, Mozart exclaimed, "Who is this that will not kiss me, when even my empress kisses me?"

No one, unfortunately, told Mozart that the kissing would ever stop. It must have seemed to the boy who was called "God's own musical instrument" that life on earth was heaven, and, accordingly, he developed but one aspect of his personality.

Only at age twenty-seven did he venture into the world to fend for himself. At that time, Baron von Grimm, once so effusive in his praises, now observed that Mozart was "too confident, too little a man of action, too much ready to succumb to his own illusions, too little *au courant*, with the ways that lead to success."

The golden-haired boy had become a musical god, but had remained an emotional Peter Pan. He just never grew up. He remained the child in the empress's arms, always laughing, always looking for the bright side, always believing that the heaven of his childhood would return, if only he could strike the right chord. He was depending on that. It was not enough.

So the No. 1 Illusion that we carry over from childhood is this: *Someone will look after me.*

Prison inmates tend to be trapped in the set of beliefs that says the world really ought to be taking care of them. They're mostly ill prepared for entry into the world. Without education, credentials, or support systems, they see no way to get what they want or need from life except to engage in ingrained antisocial behaviors. The great irony here is that being sent to prison merely reinforces the old way of thinking and the obsolete grappling styles with it. Suddenly, as if by magic, the machinations of the inmates have wrought the desired result—all their needs are being taken care of. Suddenly they're being treated like kids again. One ex-offender now on the straight and narrow confided to me that his court-appointed defender suggested a plea bargain that would result in a thirty-day sentence. "No, no," said my friend, "I'm really exhausted, I need a lot of sleep, get me sixty days."

Alas, on the way to the gate, the departing ex-offender typically entrusts the role of protector and provider to God, government programs, and assorted officials, myself included. So many students in my class, apprehensive of release, approach me for help. "I'll need a job when I get out of here," they say. "And I know you can help." I know from past experience that finding a job for an ex-offender can be both difficult and demoralizing, so I suggest another way. "You don't need a job," I reply. "What you need is an *income stream*. The bad news is that no one can *give* you that. The good news, however, is that you really can set about organizing it for yourself—and I'm going to talk about that whole subject in my last classes. In the meantime," I hand him the Wareham CLIQ—"complete this and bring it to me next week."

Corporate inmates suffer a similar problem, but it emerges from an altogether different set of circumstances. A parent-financed education dramatically extends the period of emotional and financial dependence. Credentials and connections create a deep sense of entitlement. They suffer from childhood successes that both raise expectations and deny realization that most preadult accomplishment stems from *obeisance*, whereas, in what we call the real world, most of life's real prizes go to the person prepared to break old rules or create new ones. Thus the conformist grappling style that makes a child a winner can render the adult a mindless loser who can't quite figure out what went wrong—and why he can't summon the will to slip the golden handcuffs.

I saw this in a fellow who enjoyed apparently spectacular success at college, but could only rise to a junior vice-presidency at the large corporation he joined in order to save the world. Over lunch he recounted his youthful salad days, and then misty-eyed and gazing blankly over my shoulder, he sighed heavily to no one in particular: "I *am* special, I am *still* special." In fact, he was neither as special nor as well prepared as the fine sole that lay upon his plate, and, in that moment I knew I was really hearing the voice of his mother. Mommy had not only subjugated him, but had told him that, because he was intelligent and persevering enough to get into a great college, he was "special," and, therefore, destined to greatness. Not so, dear lady, not so. The success never came. He merely married a mother surrogate, who, stubbornly believing in his potential, kept him working like a demon until the day of his heart attack.

So, here's the lesson: Childhood is over, so *depend on yourself.*

THE ENCHANTMENT OF LOCATION

When I was five years old, I enjoyed the most wonderful day of my life at a magical beach that glittered beneath the sun as my friends and I played on it. We had so much fun that when night fell I decided I would come back the next morning. That night I set my alarm and dreamed of another enchanted day.

I awoke at 6.00 A.M. and ran off to my Xanadu, only to find that it had faded. The tide was out, the beach was grimy, the day was grey, and none of my friends were around. Suddenly I saw that it wasn't the place that made the day, but my friends and the games we had played. This realization was both a disappointment and a relief. I saw that the place of my dream had not simply vanished, but that it had never, in fact, existed. At the same time I was reassured by the knowledge that my friends would be at home, kicking around the neighborhood, having fun.

The illusion that a *place* will make you happy is strongly promulgated by, among others, airlines, travel agents, and hotel chains. Want some happiness? Then buy this ticket to Florida, Honolulu, the Riviera—anywhere, except *here*. That's the thing they all agree upon—happiness is *never* here. Well, there's no commission in that, is there?

The illusion is this: we're chasing rainbows looking for a land of Oz that doesn't exist. What we're *really* seeking is the womb or the crib—and the hard reality is that *we will never get back*. We may attempt to fly away, but wherever a bird alights, its tail follows. A better strategy, according to Chandler Haste, anyway, is to see the old world in a new perspective:

> The Land of Oz came into sight
> The other day
> Or maybe it was night.
> I saw it rise and softly glimmer
> Saw it twinkle
> Watched it shimmer.
> And what I learned was this, dear friend,
> The rainbow's golden pot is now
> For this brief life is journey's end.

If we accept that muse, then the people of Oz are all about us. They may not be perfect, or even particularly glamorous, but they are the only people with whom we will ever have the opportunity to be friends. And, if we cannot befriend them, then we will never know friendship. Nor will we ever discover peace of mind.

THE FANTASY OF FAME

"If I'm a legend," said Judy Garland, near the end of her life, "then why am I so lonely?" Because, Miss Garland, you were doubtless looking for happiness outside yourself. Perhaps you were hoping to recapture the attention that you knew as a little girl. Unfortunately, in the real world, fame is no guarantee of happiness. All too often, in fact, fame merely begets misery.

Consider those who chased and found fame only to discover that in much celebrity there is much sorrow, in much glory there is much grief—Judy Garland, Ernest Hemingway, Jimi Hendrix, Janis Joplin, to name but a few. Like moths they flew to the flame, where they found that being "somebody" often involves being reduced to nobody at all. "If you ask me to play myself," said Peter Sellers, "I will not know what to do. I do not know who or what I am." Part of the problem is that fame causes a "personality" to lose its "person" and thus to become a mere commodity. "It's a crazy life," said Nancy Sinatra, talking about stardom. "You're stuck with a product—yourself."

Yet still we live in a world where men and women will literally kill for fame. Immediately after his arrest, Ronald Reagan's would-be assassin (whose name we shall choose to forget) said: "Does this mean I'll be on the six o'clock news?"

A quest for fame cannot, of course, be sated—because no one can get back to the crib. Sure, an audience can applaud, can approve, can scold, just like Mom and Dad used to. But what use is that, if, when the audience leaves, the actor remains a lonely, frightened child?

The kind of fame that comes unsought is something else again. Einstein, Schweitzer, and Freud were amused—and perhaps slightly embarrassed—by the fame their work attracted. Their real happiness sprang from accomplishment, not fame. When a starry-eyed disciple called Freud a genius, the great man quickly separated fiction from fantasy. "No," he said, "I am not a genius; I have merely made a great discovery."

THE TRICKERY OF THINGS

For years I had admired and lusted to own a rare early-model Jaguar. One day I found it in a used-car lot. Despite being twenty years old, it was a low-mileage, one-owner vehicle. The original paint job shone like the sun and the leather interior smelled of money.

And money it took to buy it—more, needless to say, than I had bargained for. I demurred for a couple of days because I already owned a very nice car. Finally, I could not restrain myself. I parted with my money, slid into the driver's seat, turned on the ignition, engaged the engine, and began, slowly, to awaken.

I don't know what I had been expecting, but I quickly discovered that it would never be found inside that car. It was heavy and cumbersome on the road, and neither the steering wheel nor the accelerator was responsive. The pleasure I had so keenly anticipated had vanished. As I rolled away from the lot, I wondered what on earth I had been thinking about and what I was doing.

Some weeks later, still pondering that question, I looked for an answer in my childhood—and found it right there. My father had been the first man in town to buy a Jaguar, and that purchase, I remember, was of some importance to him. A year later he was annoyed to see a new and sleeker model pass him at an intersection. "It's no good," I remember him saying. But the green of envy tinged his words.

So, a quarter of a century later, I tried to buy the car my father had deprecated; the same make, year, and model number—all without really knowing why. I simply felt there was some special "look" to the car. And in some ways there was, because it represented a chance for me to even a score from my childhood.

The older the boys, the bigger their toys. Many of us can and do waste a tremendous amount of our adult lives attempting, one way or another, to purchase adult versions of childhood's toys. The hope we will succeed in this doomed endeavor springs as eternal as the illusions that clever admen are so highly paid to create, and to endlessly re-create.

On this subject of owning things, Freud observed that all children, before they reach maturity, go through a phase that he called anal-erotic, which is to say that they get pleasure from holding onto their feces, thereby denying them to Mother—and thus getting even with her.

Some people never leave this immature state of development and develop accordingly what Freud called anal personalities. These are the tightwads whose lives are devoted to "holding on," to having, to saving, to hoarding—money, things, feelings, gestures, words, energy. And, yes, even feces, for hoarders frequently suffer chronic constipation.

What matters, in Freud's view, is that the major orientation toward possession occurs in the period *before* the achievement of full maturity. If it remains permanently, it is pathological.

To put it very simply, owning things for pleasure can be infantile and sick. All we're really trying to do—according to one of the greatest philosophers of our age—is reexperience the pleasure of the potty! Don't laugh. A vast number of people, particularly in America, the world's most materialistic and maternalistic society, are stuck with this problem.

They believe, on many levels, that possessing things will make them happy. And then, of course, the fear of losing what they are holding on to creates anxiety. So even just *believing* that things will make you happy can make you ill.

THE DELUSION OF THE GREEN DOOR

A frustrated fellow once offered to pay me to tell him how to speak like a corporate director. "I'm being held back by not knowing how they talk in the board room," he explained. "They talk in ways that I wouldn't be able to understand." Poor fellow. He knew they weren't speaking in tongues, yet he subscribed to this idea of mysterious things happening that were beyond his intellectual capacity.

One of life's greatest illusions is that, somewhere, behind a firmly closed door, an exclusive coterie of beautiful people is enjoying a perpetually wonderful time, doing endlessly exciting and glamorous things. If you ever find yourself thinking anything like this, then look at a transcript of the Nixon tapes. Here, as never before in history, we are made privy to the thought processes and conversations of men locked inside the Oval Office of the White House. What great wisdom can we learn from these great men? What pearls do they offer? To their horror, one hopes, and certainly to our dismay, we find that, shorn of their pubescent expletives, the emperor and all his court are worse than nude—they are downright *ordinary*. Ordinary, trite, and banal. Serves us right for believing they would be anything else.

Often, when we assume that other people, particularly the celebrated, are infinitely wiser than we are, we're simply trying to get back to childhood, where, behind their bedroom door, our parents "knew what was best for us." That belief, whether it was true or not, made us feel secure. But childhood is *over* now, and to put our faith in surrogate fathers, as many of us are unconsciously compelled to do, is to invite disappointment at the least, and all too often, tragedy.

Of Society, our old friend Oscar Wilde said: "To be in it is a bore, to be out of it a tragedy." The extent of the tragedy depends only upon your *need for approval*. Certainly it *can* be fun to go backstage as it were, but it has been my experience all over the world that backstage is merely that: a dusty, tawdry, sweaty, nowhere place where actors mostly worry about remembering their lines and what the audience thinks.

There are, of course, some very nice private clubs that you might like to join. And getting in might be easier than you think, because all you have to do is convince the members that you are *just like them*. But if you have to wear a mask to join, why bother? The best club in the world could be right behind your own front door.

THE ILLUSION OF WINNING

If and when you realize and accept that the compulsive winner is really competing for the attention of his parents, the futility of the rivalry becomes instantly apparent. On the other hand, as we have seen, losing can also be a way of winning approval. Is there *anything* we can do, then, that can't be labeled infantile? Yes, of course, there are many things. The point is that neither winning nor losing signifies immaturity *in itself*. It's our *motives* that betray us.

But how, you ask, do I know when I'm winning—or losing—for the wrong reason? Rest assured that your body *and* your mind will let you know, *if you will only listen to them*. If, for example, you've beaten the hell out of your competitors in order to earn the money to buy your wife a new car, but in the process neglected her and lost her to another, then it is obvious that you are winning for the wrong reasons—and, in reality, losing.

The pursuit of "victory" should be, I think, riveting, demanding, and, most of all, *fun*. If it isn't fun, then we might be better off losing. If you doubt this, then look at one of those "successful" corporate inmates who is compelled to hide an anguished psyche behind a mask of hyperactivity, pomposity, anger, and antacid. Poor devil. Locked in a jail of his own making, he's terrified to let anyone get close in case they discover the vacuum behind the glazed gaze. Way down deep he senses that something is seriously wrong, but he can't figure out what, and so he never knows what to do about it.

What he *should* do is what we're doing here—he should contemplate why he *really* behaves as he does, why he continues to inflict unnecessary pain upon himself. Only from there can he set about scrapping his notions of what constitutes success, tossing his old prism away, getting off the treadmill of his own infantile desires— and *setting about becoming an authentic person.* Only then will happiness start to overtake him.

THE MYTH OF MAGIC

A "magic" solution is any remedy that we hope will come from outside ourselves—from a rabbit's foot, a crystal ball, an astrological chart, a political manifesto, a controlled substance, or a bottle. All of these things promise magic solutions. None of them work. They fail because all "magical" beliefs are essentially infantile. To believe in magic is to be deluded that the world can be changed as magically as it seemed to be when you were lying in that crib, and yelled, and Mommy came running. To seek magic solutions is to chase rainbows in the hope of finding wizards. *We must perform our own magic.* And we can. We do it by refusing to believe in magic, and relying upon ourselves instead.

Belief in *any* kind of magic solution is a clear sign that one is in some kind of prison and suffering from what psychiatrists call the *delusion of reprieve.* But of course there can be no reprieve—no external solution to one's problems, magic or otherwise—because the core of the dilemma exists within one's own psyche.

The theme in everything I have just said is that we must make a conscious effort to reject *any* solution that comes from *outside of ourselves.* Our problems, remember, are etched into brain cells on the inside of our skulls. Hence the wisdom of Buddha: "There is no grace, no help, to be had from the outside."

Many people believe in promises of would-be wizards who claim they can work a little magic. Unfortunately, as Dorothy discovered, wizards are tricksters, and nowhere is this truer than when a particular wizard believes his own pitch.

The television evangelist, who promises that enthusiasm will solve all your problems and faith will move all your mountains, is typically more interested in his own glory and bank balance than your spiritual welfare. He may believe his own bromides, and his sheer exuberance may buoy you momentarily, but when he leaves, where are you? Awash in a puddle of adrenaline wanting desperately to do something, but still clueless as to what.

These kinds of people—street corner gurus and assorted "success" peddlers—are like the Wizard of Oz, tugging at *your* internal controls in order to project an image of *themselves* that is larger than life. Their illusions enthrall the child in us—the dependent child that needs to believe in magic. But this kind of magic fades the moment we reenter the real world.

The magic fades because it is *childish*. And, because it *is* childish, it is also self-defeating. We are left fluttering between elation and despair. Elation because the wizard has promised magic solutions to our problems. Despair because he has left us even more dependent than he found us. Big Daddy has gone off to charm another hall full of children who never grew up. Now *we* are alone again, and the world is as problematical and frightening as ever it was. I think I hear the wicked witch coming again. Who will save me? How will I ever get to Oz now? Help!

Relax, my friend, a dose of rationality will save the day.

CHAPTER 8

How to Revise Your Alibi
& Overturn Your Conviction

No man remains quite what he was when he recognizes himself.

—Thomas Mann

One of literature's great ironies lies in the story of Oedipus Rex, who hears from the Delphic Oracle that he is fated to slay his father and marry his mother. Shocked by this prophecy, and determined to protect those whom he thinks are his parents, Oedipus flees Corinth.

Though unaware of the fact, Oedipus is actually an adopted child and ignorant of the identities of his true parents. At a crossroad in his travels Oedipus meets, quarrels with, and kills a "stranger"— his own father.

Oedipus subsequently wins the right to become King and husband to Jocasta, the queen of Thebes. Some years later, Jocasta and Oedipus discover that they are, in fact, mother and son. Faced with this knowledge, Jocasta commits suicide and Oedipus blinds himself.

The irony in the tale lies in the admonition inscribed above the Delphic Oracle's door. *Know Thyself* was the cryptic qualifier to every oracular proclamation. Oedipus failed to heed this warning, and, not knowing his own identity, he was unconsciously compelled to fulfill the oracle's tragic prophecy. In attempting to flee his past, he merely carried it along with him.

Most people do much the same. We are enslaved by the past until we examine it closely enough to discover who we really are, what we are really doing, and who is really pulling the strings.

If four prison walls confine you it's hard to escape the realization that you're doing something wrong. It's harder for outwardly success-

131

ful individuals to objectively consider the problem areas of their lives. But when they summon the courage to examine the painful areas of their lives with an open mind—and then set about connecting the dots—they might be in for a surprise.

To know thyself is much, much easier said than done, for the very simple reason that self-knowledge is routinely denied to us by our own thought processes. What we *can* do, however, as a highly practical second step once we have rejected the illusion of autonomy, is to analyze our own lives. When we do this, we draw the curtain in order to discover the wizard, along with the rest of the characters, and the whole script. This means consciously identifying the values, desires, and injunctions that make up the value system, psychic contract, grappling style, and other internal forces that govern our behaviors.

Once you truly know your own script, you can then set about *acting to change it*—you can choose, for the first time, how to run and live your own life. You may, of course, decide that you *want* to stay "on script"—to live according to the values and ideals you were raised with. That's fine, too, because, now, even this decision represents your own conscious, autonomous, rational choice.

No one book can, of course, tell everyone everything they need to know in order to discover their programming. Psychoanalysts making hundreds of dollars an hour for discovering scripts will avow that such discoveries take many years. For a genuinely curious person, however, a short spell of self-analysis often yields amazingly fast insights. So, I trust you didn't skip the Wareham CLIQ (Condensed Life Insight Questionnaire). If you haven't done so, go back to page 27 and do it now. Even then you may have compromised your capacity for candor if you've read this far. Answer as spontaneously as possible and return right here to learn what's behind the curtain.

Analyze Your Penitentiary

Okay, then. My lifetime of experience with the CLIQ has taught me that the responses are infinitely more revealing and originate from much deeper places than the test taker realizes. To cite an example, I was once asked to advise on whether a particular executive should be fired. Upon completion of the CLIQ one response caught my eye. The sentence stem read, "I become depressed . . ." (the poignant response encapsulated the precise state of his life) ". . . when autumn comes to an end." That executive was a burned-out shell. Way down deep he knew that the autumn of his life was about to end. The point is to take your responses seriously and not discount them.

For convenience sake, let's refer to the questions as Q1, Q2, and so on, and your personal responses as R1, R2, R3 and so on. In the table below, copy your responses to the following questions:

PRISON	Q#	RESPONSE
Prime Parental Injunction, (PPIN)	4	My parents always told me I should
Embedded Expectation	11	I was expected to become
Guru	15 a	The person who most influenced the development of my personality was
Gospel	15b	who taught me
Prism	12	The best measure of personal success is
Financial Comfort Level, (FCL)	21	Realistically, to enjoy a satisfactory lifestyle I need an annual income of approximately
Foreboding	35	My greatest fear
Focus	17	The main driving force in my life is
Snapshot	40	Job _____ Finances _____ Fulfillment _____ Relationships _____

What you are looking at here, my friend, is the cage—or prison—of your own beliefs. The name of your *Guru*—R15a—and the *Focus* of your current life—R17—may be accurate, but other responses all reflect the values that have shaped and are shaping your life.

There is also enough information contained in this set of responses to estimate the terms of your psychic contract. And to begin thinking about whether you are—or want to be—a winner, loser, or at-leaster on your own terms or somebody else's.

First, however, let's look a little more closely at your responses and what they might mean.

➤ Your *Prime Parental Injunction* or *PPIN*—R4—and your *Embedded Expectation*—R11—are key aspects of your psychic contract. Both items relate to the life that your parents ordained for you. The PPIN is intrinsic to the insistent voice of conscience, and presses you on. The embedded expectation attaches to your hopes and fears, and pulls in directions you might not always want to go. Carl Upchurch, in his brilliant book *Convicted in the Womb*, recalls the PPIN and embedded expectation that his single-parent, drug-addict mother bequeathed him: "You'll never amount to nothing, you'll be a thief or a bum or a dope dealer, you ain't worth a shit."

To my surprise, the PPINs and embedded expectations of *most* pupils in my class were to get educated and join the ranks of doctors, accountants, lawyers, athletes, and film makers. In fact, these ambitious expectations were mostly instilled by earnest single-parent mothers and failed to overpower an aberrant—and mostly absent— father's criminal example. By setting the bar so high, however, the odds of failure were increased so that subsequent failure merely compounded an already injured sense of self-esteem.

Compare that with the expectation of one of the world's greatest painters. "My father told me that if I joined the army I'd become a general and if I joined the priesthood they'd make me Pope. In fact, I became an artist and wound up as Picasso." The irony here is that Pablo Picasso's father was himself an outstanding painter of his day, and therefore a superb role model.

We base many of our key decisions today upon the past as we saw it then. Our early lives become continuing dramas, and we go on playing roles—clown, witch, loser, tough guy, Mama's boy, to name a few—assigned to us by our parents. If you're one of those who chose to "rebel," then your conscience has probably inflicted some punishment upon you, or even sabotaged your efforts. Consider the case of Tycoon Tom. "It wasn't possible for me to catch my father's attention," said Tom. "He was always too involved in his business to be bothered with me." Then Tom remembered that there had, in fact, been one time when his father had shown special interest in him. "It was when I ran away from home," said Tom. "He came after me then." Suddenly Tom realized something important. "I've been running away from home ever since," he whispered. First, Tom left the town of his birth, then the country. Pretty soon he'd lived in some twenty cities all over the world. Only now does he know *why*.

Few people run away from home. Most people, however, are attempting, one way or another, to catch the attention of their parents, thereby recapturing, they hope, the fleeting bliss of childhood love and attention. The chronic storyteller who feels compelled to tell and retell tired tales is usually seeking parental affection. In fact, all approval-seeking behavior—whether of the compulsive winner or the compulsive show-off reflects just that: a chronic desire for parental approbation. And what is too often overlooked is that many people try to win approval by *conforming*—by living mindless automatons' lives. Only by recognizing our own approval-seeking ploys can we choose to give them up. Until then we are compelled to repeat them.

By the mere accident of birth, our parents fix our place in society and then indoctrinate us with the values of that culture. Accordingly, social mores account for much mindless individual behavior. The Greeks, for example, perceiving Socrates to be a traitor, proffered him hemlock. The Victorians, thinking Sigmund Freud a lecher, pelted him with rotten fruit. A celebrity-infatuated society, projecting greatness onto a celluloid idol, elected Ronald Reagan president. Our parents instill *social* values into us, so that a whole "cultural overlay" becomes part of us, reinforcing most of our key values and goals, along with our thinking processes. We are normally as oblivious to the social influences that shape our lives as is a fish to the water from which it takes oxygen. We assume that *our* culture is the normal one—and usually also that it is the best one—and thus we take its influences for granted. In fact, as anthropologist Edward Hall observed, entire societies can become crazy and dysfunctional, which is in part why so many people "choose" crazy scripts.

➤ Your *Prism*—R12—is the lens through which you view your goals and achievements. You probably take your prism very seriously, without quite realizing the extent to which it relates to your PPIN. In fact, the prism is typically a conscious rationalization of a PPIN you believe you have forgotten or disregarded. The flawed overachiever's prism is recognition, status, and lifestyle. The authentic achiever's prism is accomplishment and contribution. The typical executive's prism is family and career. Paradoxically, perhaps, the prison inmate's prism is often associated with the qualities of *character*—happiness, contentment, wisdom.

➤ Your *Guru*—R15a—is or was a key figure who shared his *Gospel*—R15b—, which you likely uncritically absorbed. For many, a parent may also be the guru. Executives mostly cite their fathers. Prison inmates almost always cite their mothers. Overachievers are more likely to cite a nonparental role model, someone who satisfied missing inner needs—or know-how—and who gave a special kind of emotional support that a parent never could. It is fairly common to model an entire life on the life of a guru and his gospel.

➤ Your *Financial Comfort Level* or *FCL*—R21—almost certainly relates to your embedded expectation, your PPIN, and your prism. We might say that it is the dollar value that attaches to your psychic contract. The income or status level attained by your family—and, in particular, by your most dominant parent—is likely to represent your own unconscious "comfort level," both physical and psychic. Your comfort level will almost certainly define the place in the social strata that you will spend most of your life trying to attain or maintain. This psychic destination is part of the psychic contract that we discussed earlier. If you "arrive" you are a "winner," and if you fail to make the grade then you are, of course, a loser. One way or another, most of the time, the FCL directly relates to the psychic contract. Apparent exceptions to the rule include people who:

1. pride themselves on not being as driven by the almighty dollar as their parents were, set a low FCL yet still manage to outperform the parent by making a career in a higher-status role, perhaps as an artist, poet, or philosopher.

2. deliberately—or unconsciously—fall into something like poverty as a way of getting even with a demanding parent.

3. Attempt to erase the perceived ignominy of humble origins by becoming *visibly* "successful."

I was initially surprised to discover that almost one third of my prison class cited a financial comfort level of $100,000 per annum or higher. Currently, that would place them on a par with many mid-level managers and executives. In fact, such an income is relatively common enough among drug dealers, so the aspiration is not entirely unrealistic, as long as one is prepared to operate outside the law.

➤ Your *Foreboding*—R35—is often a key element of your mental prison. I remember reading of a gang of burglars who, armed with inside advice from a dishonest security company employee, broke into homes with recently installed safes and demanded that the owner open his safe and hand over his valuables. If the owner demurred, the thieves would threaten to apply a bolt cutter to his toes. Unfortunately, some of those safes were still awaiting installation so many toes were needlessly removed. In that case, the moment a fearful homeowner ordered a safe he *increased* his likelihood of being robbed. So, too, in our own lives, the strategies we devise to protect us from our greatest fear often actually attract it. The most common foreboding among bootstrapping executives is that they may fall back into the underclass from whence they sprang. The common foreboding among prison inmates is that they may never be able to earn a sufficient income within the law.

➤ Your *Focus*—R17—reflects where you are putting your energy and effort right now. It would make sense to work upon the areas of life that are sources of grief. In truth, too many people merely waste their time reacting to the terms of the psychic contract to live the life of their dreams. Or they engage in *perseveration*—the pursuit of an activity long after the need for that activity has passed. Many career criminals fall into this category. So, too, with the many successful executives who go on chasing a dollar long after their pockets are full.

As you would expect, the focus for outstanding executives is for on-the-job performance. They want to show achievement and win recognition. The not-so-driven put the focus on family and career. They want to enjoy job security and a balanced life. These people are generally managers rather than leaders. The focus for prison inmates—or at least the focus that they recorded on the Wareham

CLIQ—is to draw close to God and family. In fact, God accounted for a whopping 30 percent of all responses and family collected most of the balance. Inmates are in a potentially dangerous environment and are unemployed (or enjoying absolute security of employment!), so God offers a shield against danger, along with the prospect of survival and ultimate happiness. Just the same, I was struck by the fact that relatively few inmates focused upon how best to effect a successful reentry to the outside world.

➤ Your *Snapshot*—R40—summarizes your satisfaction level in four key areas of your life. Many executives report high ratings on finances but mediocre ratings on job, fulfillment, and relationships. The inference is that they've been making good on their psychic contracts, but are unhappy because they're imprisoned in unfulfilling roles that leave little time for relationships. Prison inmates, on the other hand, report rotten ratings on job and finances, and higher ratings on personal fulfillment and relationships. Prison life takes care of immediate financial needs, the real issues of life become more apparent, and as we have seen, the succor of friendship and spirituality more abundant.

At this point, it might be useful to consider some actual examples—with name changes, of course—from my files.

LANGSTON STRETCH

Langston	Q#	45, Classic overachiever
PPIN	4	My parents always told me I should stop "gonna do it" and do it—I listened.
Embedded Expectation	11	I was expected to become an outstanding success.
Guru	15a	The person who most influenced the development of my personality was a former boss.
Gospel	15b	who taught me how to muscle-build an organization.

Prism	12	The best measure of personal success is being at one with yourself and your family and doing exactly what you and they want.
$$$ Comfort Level	21	Realistically, to enjoy a satisfactory lifestyle I need an annual income of approximately half a million dollars.
Foreboding	35	My greatest fear—I'm frightened of nothing.
Focus	17	The main driving force in my life is the need to be successful.
Snapshot	40	Job 7 Finances 9 Fulfillment 7 Relationships 7

Langston, whose charm masks an intense need to obliterate his competitors, is well on the way to the success and recognition he dreams about. The PPIN was affixed to his Contrarian heart by a challenging blue-collar father. Langston nonetheless saw the wisdom in the message and resolved to show the old man a thing or two. A quick learner, he found a mentor and again listened closely. The half-million-dollar income is highly realistic given his talent, drive, and discipline. He says he's frightened of nothing, but in fact, like most overachievers he's pricked by the fear of failure, loss of respect, and return to his humble origins. Despite the nod in the direction of his family, Langston is clearly focused upon realizing his ambition to become an outstanding success.

JOAN GLITTER

Joan	Q#	30, single parent, wannabe business leader
PPIN	4	My parents always told me I should think before I speak.
Embedded Expectation	11	I was expected to become a big success in business.
Guru	15a	The person who most influenced the development of my personality was my brother.

Gospel	15b	who taught me to stand up for myself.
Prism	12	The best measure of personal success is wealth.
$$$ Comfort Level	21	Realistically, to enjoy a satisfactory lifestyle I need an annual income of approximately $200,000.00.
Foreboding	35	My greatest fear is of not succeeding in life.
Focus	17	The main driving force in my life is my children.
Snapshot	40	Job 6 Finances 3 Fulfillment 7 Relationships 5

Joan, a very attractive single mother, is highly frustrated in a middle-management role, but holds the expectation of becoming a big success, which, according to her prism means to acquire great wealth. In fact, unless she wins the lottery—or the marriage sweepstakes—even the $200,000 salary will remain out of reach. She is so unrealistic and has set the bar so high that a crippling fear of failure necessarily follows. The focus of Joan's life—her children—is laudable, but, unfortunately, a further impediment to winning the money she thinks that life somehow owes her. The snapshot clearly reflects an unhappy situation. All things considered, Joan's think-before-you-speak PPIN probably reflects a parental wish to instill a little realism.

FRANK YEARNER

Frank	Q#	22-year-old armed drug dealer and wannabe mogul
PPIN	4	My parents always told me I should be a leader not a follower.
Embedded Expectation	11	I was expected to become a great writer and film director.
Guru	15a	The person who most influenced the development of my personality was my mother.

Gospel	15b	who taught me that setting goals was the key to success.
Prism	12	The best measure of personal success is contentment.
$$$ Comfort Level	21	Realistically, to enjoy a satisfactory lifestyle I need an annual income of approximately $50,000.00.
Foreboding	35	My greatest fear is coming up short and failing at life.
Focus	17	The main driving force in my life is my finances.
Snapshot	40	Job 1 Finances 1 Fulfillment 6 Relationships 8

In our opening session, Frank regaled the class with great bravado, telling of how he got picked up on a street corner, high on drugs, and carrying "a burner." These days, he's softly spoken, charming, and keen to learn. Like so many in my class, Frank has been overwhelmed by the combination of an ambitious PPIN and unrealistic embedded expectation. Let's be honest: it takes great effort and long hours to become a writer or film director, so earning even the modest income needed to survive while pursuing such an ambition can seem like a daunting task. It is even more difficult however for *anyone* to become a *great* writer or film director. Frank's mother was right to teach the importance of goals. Unfortunately, she apparently failed to stress the importance of realistic milestones along the way. Frustrated by his dreams and tormented by his fear of failure, Frank turned to drugs, then tried to deal them, to which end, given his youth and emotional fragility, the "burner" became a necessary appendage. At this point, the only bright spot in his snapshot seems to be his fiancée.

How to Overturn Your Conviction

Overturning your conviction is easy. Since the original prosecuting team was your own ambivalent inner demons, it will now be perfectly okay to assign yourself the role of judge at your own special appeal. So simply rule in favor of the defense and rewrite your psychic contract—for that's the covenant, more than just about anything else, that has you imprisoned. Your jailer is the particular pact—which exists only in the mind—and for you defines success or failure. Here are some examples:

- ➤ A winner's PPIN, Embedded Expectation, and Prism are in harmony—and the Lifestyle eclipses that of the childhood home.

- ➤ An at-leaster's PPIN, Embedded Expectation, and Prism are in harmony—but the Lifestyle falls short of that of the childhood home.

- ➤ A loser's Lifestyle falls way short of the childhood home and Embedded Expectations. The Prism becomes one of bitterness or cynicism—or is dissolved in alcohol or drugs.

The trouble with these definitions, of course, is that the *mindless* fulfillment of a psychic contract is *never* truly fulfilling. As long as we are running our lives on other people's programs we are prisoners. Or, as Erich Fromm put it, "Whether or not we are aware of it, there is nothing of which we are more ashamed than of not being ourselves."

The net effect is that even a so-called winner may be imprisoned by a psychic contract. His predicament—like that of any psychic contract inmate—can be likened to an innocent person who turns himself over to the authorities for a crime he didn't commit. His mistake is the failure to live his own life on his own terms. So think about those core values.

Does your PPIN reflect an accurate statement? Is it true, for instance, that one should always behave or be polite? Or work hard? Or achieve? Or trust in God? The answer in each case is that it all depends on what kind of a life you want for yourself.

The same is true, of course, of your embedded expectation—which might not, in fact, be yours at all. Most people really do live their lives according to other people's expectations. The lucky ones climb the ladder of success and fail to notice, even at the end of their lives that it has been leaning against the wrong wall. Instead, they merely feel the empty kind of cynical ache in the heart that Peggy Lee captured so well in her signature song, "Is That All There Is?" Don't let that happen to you.

Think about the guru and his gospel. It might just be time to put that person and philosophy out of your life and to live according to an entirely personal philosophy. The Buddhists say, "When you meet your Buddha on the road, kill him." They're not urging actual homicide. They're merely saying to learn whatever it is that a particular mentor has to teach, and then move on with your own spiritual journey and discover your own wisdom.

How accurate is that prism? If you have defined success in terms of winning and achievement you might just be sacrificing other elements of a happy life. If your prism is security you might end up serving a life sentence in an unsatisfying but secure job. If your concern is merely happiness, you might be missing the value of contributing to others.

THE MONKEY TRAP

The crucial underlying element in the financial comfort level—R8—is usually the psychic contract. The "how" typically precludes contemplation of "what" we should really be doing. We *need* a certain income because we have been programmed to *want* a certain lifestyle. Lifestyle needs can tempt innocent people into drug-dealing roles; corporate inmates and countless executives are trapped on the lifestyle treadmill, slaving to foot the bill. They typically fall into this trap early in life and never manage to find a way out of it. They dedicate a lifetime to keeping up with the Joneses. At the end of the journey they have either failed miserably or succeeded miserably.

One way to think about this whole issue is to contemplate the method used to entrap the African monkey. A large nut is placed inside a small cage. The monkey sees and scents the nut, inserts its paw through a small opening in the bottom of the cage, and grasps the bait. But when the monkey's paw is holding the nut, it is too large to withdraw. To escape the trap, the monkey must let go of the nut. Being almost human, however, the monkey is too greedy to let go, and thus becomes the guard to its own imprisonment.

Real maturity usually begins with a decision to live within one's means. This doesn't mean accepting less than the life we want. In fact, the decision to take a step down is often the first step toward the life we *really* want. Reducing the Financial Comfort Level can create an otherwise unattainable commodity: the time we need to pursue our own best interests.

Sometimes, we can leave the Financial Comfort Level untouched and use a little creativity to pursue our dreams. A friend, a gifted photographer, was explaining how she was being held back in her dream of becoming and earning a reputation as a fine artist by the need to make a living selling commercial family portraits. The conundrum, she explained, was that a family understandably wants to purchase essentially flattering portraits, whereas the best photos from a fine arts perspective often expose underlying suffering or vanity. In fact, she was too close to her own situation to realize that she was perfectly placed to make good on her dream. These days whenever she visits a family to shoot portraits she assures them that they'll get exactly the photos they want. She then goes on to explain that she'd like to include a portrait of their choosing—along with something "moody and different" of her choosing—in a personal project that she's currently working on. Human nature being what it is, everyone has so far agreed to be in the book—and a publisher just loves the whole idea. So now the dream of becoming a true artist is in the process of realization. All it took was a little thinking, along with the realization that her everyday circumstances represented a unique opportunity, not an insurmountable impediment.

The key rule concerning forebodings is to *focus upon what is under our control and to forget about everything else.* Forebodings come in three categories: calamities that will never happen, misfortunes that worrying just might attract, and things that will probably never happen. Actually, nearly all fears and forebodings fall into that latter group. Most people worry about losing loved ones, or losing their jobs, or becoming poverty-stricken and dying in the streets. Overachievers fret over failure instead of heeding the observation of the poet, Rudyard Kipling, that triumph and disaster are both imposters. The truth of the matter is that the worst thing that might happen almost never does, and that even when it does, we usually find that the apprehension is infinitely worse than the actual tragedy.

As to the actual snapshot, well, if everything is a 10, then, congratulations, your life is order and you're doing fine. And if after examining your core values you make a conscious and rational decision that you do, indeed, *want* to fulfill your "family destiny," then that is something else again. The conscious act of reaching that decision dissolves the script. What was someone else's program is now your free choice. You cease to be a zombie and start to live your own life.

OBSTACLES AND OPORTUNITIES

If, like most people, one or more of the elements is falling short for you, then you're not getting what you want from life, so it might be helpful to analyze the cause of the problem. For openers, let's consider obstacles to success and alibis for ultimate failure.

CALIBRATION	Q#	SENTENCE STEM
Cross	33	I suffered most from.
Albatross*	24	I feel I am being held back by.
Turning Point	13	The defining moment of my life.
Sisyphusian Stone	19	I am trying to overcome.
Paternal Vacuum	6	If only my father.
Maternal Vacuum	9	If only my mother.

➤ The *Cross*—R33—is an impediment bequeathed relatively early in life. Sometimes it is real, sometimes it is created by the imagination.

➤ The *Turning point*—R13—may be positive or negative. Winning executives often cite the award of a particular promotion, losers typically complain of missing out on one and falling into a downward spiral. Getting arrested is often the tragic turning point for many inmates. Needless to say, it takes tremendous courage and perseverance to overcome the trauma of formal criminalization.

➤ The *Albatross*—R24—is a potentially lifelong encumbrance concocted in the mind by people who cannot imagine themselves able to address life's challenges. The burden seems real enough

---

*A huge bird, the killing of which, myth warns, will result in one's own death, a fate one can only escape by hanging the bird's corpse around one's neck and leaving it there.

and other people can also be persuaded to believe in it. The albatross comes in many forms: lack of education, higher education, or higher-status education; lack of income or capital; outsider status or lack of opportunity; invalid parent or unhelpful spouse; being too young or too old; glass ceilings or lack of connections; criminal record or inappropriately tinted epidermis—well, you get the picture.

➤ As mentioned, Sisyphus was condemned by the gods to go on for all eternity pushing a stone up a mountain only to have it roll back down. For our purposes, the rolling of a *Sisyphusian Stone*—R19—is a perpetual diversion. Those who roll it win praise for trying, but they never truly intend to win. They don't believe they can, so they never give it their all. If they didn't have that stone to roll, they'd be at a loss for an excuse.

➤ The *Parental Vacuum—Paternal* R6 *or Maternal* R9—represents an ache in the heart concerning one's parents that typically continues to affect current behavior. It possibly reflects what Sigmund Freud called "the unfinished business of childhood."

Let's consider some actual examples.

EDDIE JUMP

Eddie	Q#	30, financial advisor
Cross	33	I suffered most from prostituting myself for my current employer.
Albatross	24	I feel I am being held back by a boss who doesn't realize what I've done for the company.
Turning Point	13	The defining moment of my life was meeting the mentor who changed my life by sponsoring me into the finance industry.
Sisyphusian Stone	19	I am trying to overcome my urge to quit.

Paternal Vacuum	6	If only my father could understand my needs and ambitions.
Maternal Vacuum	9	If only my mother had stayed young forever.

Eddie, who we met earlier, is barely thirty years old and has been earning a quarter of a million dollars a year and is complaining about that not being enough. He completed the CLIQ just one week before getting fired. In fact, Eddie's mentor may have done him a bad turn by introducing him to the big-bucks world. His cross, he says, is the need to prostitute himself, and his albatross is an unsympathetic boss. His heart is telling him to quit but he can't because he's addicted to the money. No wonder his father—a blue-collar worker who never made more than thirty thousand dollars a year—doesn't understand Eddie's needs. The maternal vacuum suggests that Eddie is something of a compulsive seducer. All things considered, Eddie's values constitute a major impediment to his own good time.

RAFAEL PHOENIX

Rafael	Q#	36-year-old former long-term hustler, soon to be released
Cross	33	I suffered most from the beatings of my stepfather.
Albatross	24	I feel I am being held back by my stubbornness, but I'm working on it.
Turning point	13	The defining moment of my life was getting arrested and then seeing the light.
Sisyphusian Stone	19	I am trying to overcome my fear of success.
Paternal Vacuum	6	If only my father had been around when I needed him I mightn't have had to learn things the hard way.
Maternal Vacuum	9	If only my mother hadn't smothered me so much I might not have rebelled.

Rafael, on the other hand, was released from prison at about the same time that Eddie got fired. Rafael completed the CLIQ while still incarcerated. From the look of his responses he really has seen something worthwhile. His take on life looks pretty good, so his alibis are mostly sound. Fortunately, the cross of a brutal stepfather is in the past, or so one hopes, and the albatross of stubbornness—Rafael was a classic Contrarian—is giving way to counseling and insight. The Sisyphusian stone, fear of success, could be around for a long time, but at least Rafael is aware of the problem. The parental vacuums are essentially blame-shifters— especially in the case of the caring mother—but all things considered, Rafael is making great progress and could wind up a winner.

DIANNE FINE

Dianne	Q#	33, executive
Cross	33	I suffered most from the loss of my father.
Albatross	24	I feel I am being held back by shadows and assumptions, all inflicted by me.
Turning Point	13	The defining moment of my life was to pursue my M.B.A. and my full potential.
Sisyphusian Stone	19	I am trying to overcome the fact that I am too strong-minded on some issues.
Paternal Vacuum	6	If only my father had looked after himself better.
Maternal Vacuum	9	If only my mother would live forever.

Dianne's father was her role model. Now that he has passed on she has taken charge of her own life and is making no excuses. Her turning point is decidedly positive and reflects strong self-improvement needs. She shows insight into a tendency to be too opinionated. The parental vacuums both reflect positive love and affection. Dianne is clearly well-adjusted. Since completing the CLIQ she has been appointed leader of a key business unit and is turning in strong results.

Wayne	Q#	55, franchise operator
Cross	33	I suffered most from my high integrity.
Albatross	24	I feel I am being held back by business partners who don't understand the market situation.
Turning Point	13	The defining moment of my life was when the market turned sour.
Sisyphusian Stone	19	I am trying to overcome my resentment of the situation.
Paternal Vacuum	6	If only my father hadn't been an alcoholic.
Maternal Vacuum	9	If only my mother hadn't smoked she'd still be alive.

Wayne, an ultimate loser, completed the CLIQ prior to getting fired. In fact, for him, that termination proved something of a financial windfall, for it saddled his partners with the trail of creditors he left behind. The parental vacuum suggests a dysfunctional home. The cross of "high integrity," a common alibi among failing executives, in fact suggests highly porous principles. A classic Obedio and blame-shifter, Wayne cites a "sour market" as his turning point, then claims as his albatross the very same business partners who in fact financed him and picked up after him. Wayne's Sisyphusian stone, resentment, is nonsensical, but vintage Obedio: he not only totally denies responsibility for the situation that he wrought, he also manages to extract victim status for himself.

How to Create an Elegant Alibi

Concocting alibis and excuses is a favorite human pastime. Such justifications can be perfectly legitimate: life really is unfair. Poverty, child-abuse, lack of educational opportunities—not to mention racism and dirty politics—are all real. So if a toxic or dysfunctional parent let you down, then your life may well have been adversely affected. So study your responses to the two parental vacuums—R6 and R9—and think about how these voids may have weakened you and impeded your progress through life. Then go through the same exercise again, and reflect upon how that very same parental vacuum may actually have strengthened you.

If your turning point—R13—really was a nasty trauma—which for the moment is what inclusion within the above table implies—then your self-esteem was almost certainly impaired. It is important to fully realize, however, that problems with one's parents and childhood traumas happened in the past. We can complain, and foment, and storm, and rail, and point the finger, but we can never alter what has already happened. As long as we merely agonize over whatever egregious misfortunes befell us, we remain shackled to unhappiness. We can either stay stuck in the past or we can unfetter ourselves and get on with our lives.

The function of the cross and the albatross, for many people, is to provide immediate proof of victim status. No other alibi for failure need therefore be offered. However, people who talk about having a cross to bear often fail to appreciate that just because they have acquired one does not mean that they do not *have* to bear it. Crosses and albatrosses can often be discarded at will or, better yet, transformed into gifts.

My own cross used to be a nasty stutter. At twenty-four years of age, however, I suddenly decided I'd had enough of remaining grotesquely mute and joined a public speaking club. Two years later I won every national prize worth having, and then went on to earn top dollar as a business lecturer. Nowadays, I teach public speaking to senior executives in need of polishing and to prison inmates in need of parole. In the end, my impediment turned out to be something of a gift. In order to face down my fears I was forced to reinvent myself along with my breathing.

So take a hard-headed, unsympathetic look at your own responses and answer this question: Am I kidding myself, or what?

Now, with your alibi out of the way, you're pretty well ready to create the life of your dreams—so let's think about that right now.

CHAPTER 9

How to Create the Life of Your Dreams
A 7-Step Formula

O God! I could be bound in a nutshell,
                        and count myself a king of infinite space,
were it not that I have bad dreams.

—William Shakespeare, *Hamlet*

"My dream is to become a porn star," said Damon, "because I'd enjoy making love to women for money."

This apparently asinine expression of desire proved to be the most constructive offering from a class of thirty souls on the subject of "My Dream."

Some of the inmates expressed the yearning to earn a decent income. Others spoke of "living comfortably." Some dreamed of inhabiting a real home rather than a homeless shelter. Several vowed to pursue the vision of "never returning to Rikers." At the end of the session, however, Damon came the closest to giving the kind of answer I was hoping to hear.

Then the last speaker, a Contrario to the core, confided the underlying communal secret, "I ain't got no dream," he said. That confession came as no surprise. Bear in mind that there is practically no difference between the PPINs and embedded expectations of prison inmates and corporate executives. Both groups are enjoined to work hard and become professionals. The difference, of course, is that the inmates receive neither the education nor the support to pursue that dream, so their visions are fantasies that inevitably turn sour. They quit on their dreams to protect themselves from the pain of further failure.

Okay then, it's time for the rubber to hit the road, I'm thinking. But what should I tell a prison class about dreams? The same that I would tell any other audience. So here I go:

151

In Arthur Miller's *Death of a Salesman*, a protagonist at Willy Loman's funeral observes that a salesman has got to dream. In fact, we all do. Life is hard without a dream to invest life with purpose and meaning. Without a vision of where you'd like to be, you'll probably wind up somewhere you don't like. Not having a goal may inadvertently deny you the opportunity to become the self-fulfilled person you could—and should—have been. By my reckoning there are five letters in the word dream.

D is for Depth. Your dream should relate to your deepest desires. Don't try to live someone else's dream. If you don't have a dream right now, then look into your heart and reflect upon your talents. Martha Graham, the dancer, said "There is a vitality, a life force, a quickening that is translated through you into action, and because there is only one of you, this expression is unique. If you block it, it will never exist through any other medium and will be lost." You can also extract a dream from the rotten hand that life may have dealt you. You could dream, for example, of showing other people how to overcome adversity, or to deal with it with dignity. Many of the greatest dreams have stemmed from the need to surmount suffering.

R is for Reach. The philosopher Goethe said, "Dream no small dreams, for they have no power to stir men's hearts." I've personally always found it easier to pursue a big dream in the big leagues. That's why I'm out here in this class with you guys. I figure there may be more difficult audiences in the nation, but the Rikers crowd inspires special respect. Remember this, too, getting out and staying out of Rikers is an enormous achievement, something to be proud of—and *you* can do it. But don't cast your dreams in the negative. If you dream of *not* coming back to prison, you set your mind in a negative stance. Better to rephrase the entire dream. Say, instead, "I'm going to become a productive, contributing, tax-paying citizen." Not too many of those people ever return to prison. That's because savvy judges don't want to interrupt the capacity of truly industrious citizens to contribute to the common coffers.

E is for Explicit. If you can't name it you can't claim it. A *vague* idea of what you *might* like to do won't hack it. So set yourself a goal that is highly specific. When I was trying to overcome my stutter I set myself the goal of winning the most prestigious oratory competition in the country within two years. Goals and deadlines are vital. A goal is a dream with a deadline. When you say exactly what you want and then go on to set a deadline, the brain suddenly begins to take command. It wakes you, focuses you, and keeps you going. You're suddenly alive in every cell of your being. You suddenly possess more insight than you'd ever imagined possible.

A is for Action. If you have a dream and post it on your mirror, and then do nothing, well, nothing is what will happen. We have to forge ahead. We have to summon the courage to put one foot in front of the other. But when we do, we find ourselves in for a surprise. The writer Henry David Thoreau said that if one advances confidently in the direction of his dreams and endeavors to live the life that he has imagined, he will meet with a success unexpected in the common hours.

M is for Milestones. A really big dream can sometimes seem a little overwhelming, so it's also important to cut it down to bite-sized chunks in the form of a realistic plan and a series of challenging but achievable milestones. This way, you'll be able to monitor your progress and know that you're on track. The occasional setback won't seem so bad, and you'll find a way to overcome it or work around it. Each success will build your morale and resolve to continue striving.

Now, since I'm on my feet talking to a bunch of guys, some of whom might just be starting to look like serious dreamers, I'd like to add a couple more letters to the word *dream* and turn it into *dreamer*.

This second **E is for Evaluation.** Often, after jumping into the fray, we see things that we could never see before. New opportunities may open up, unanticipated obstacles may appear, so we may want to recalibrate the milestones, perhaps even the dream. We never give up—we simply make an adjustment to maintain spirit and momentum.

The final **R is for Rejoicing.** It is important to celebrate our successes. To go out and party, burn a candle, have a nice dinner, raise a glass, and toast the accomplishment of a milestone achieved, and the people who contributed to making it all happen. And at the close of that celebration, we look forward to the next challenge.

Now, as to your dream of becoming a porn star, Damon. Well, let me say right away that it has the virtue of tapping what you believe are your talents, and of setting a challenge, and of being reasonably specific. I mean you know the industry, and you know that you want to be an honest-to-god star, too, right? My guess, however, is that this dream—this potential nightmare, actually—is coming from a deeper place than you realize. My hunch is that you are actually expressing the need to find some authentic love in your life. I figure, also, that you've been so badly hurt at various points along the way and are confusing love with sex, hoping to use sex as a means to treat the wounds to your self-esteem. But that's for you to say. If you'd like to talk about a real dream, rather than merely another of the essentially destructive fantasies that have brought you to this place, then maybe we can talk about it later.

The Stuff that Dreams Are Made Of

So that was the speech. I guess I could have added that our dreams are inexorably linked to both imprisonment and freedom. An unrealistic dream can be turned into a nightmarish prison. A realistic dream, on the other hand, has the power to set us free in every way imaginable.

Let's take a quick look at the stuff that dreams are made of, the collection of keys that lead to freedom and make our dreams come true.

Keys to Freedom	Q#	Sentence Stem
Turning Point	13	The defining moment of my life
Game	10	As a child I loved to
Milestone	34	My most significant achievement

Disposition	1	I am very
Talisman	26	The thing I like about myself is
Gift	2	My greatest talent
Calling	36	If I could have any career I'd be a
Dream	39	My dream
Wish	38	I wish

As noted previously, more than two thirds of prison inmates testify to a negative turning point in their lives, and in nearly half the cases it's getting arrested. By comparison, better than 95 percent of executives record positive turning points. What many of both types fail to realize is that we can *choose* to create turning points in our lives. Some years ago I decided to make a change in my own life. The first thing I did— or maybe the second, actually—was to change my birthday. I was an unwanted child and that day which should have been so special always seemed to create anxiety and tension. So I selected another date, one that held special meaning for me, and made a conscious decision to expunge the first one from my memory. Since that time, I've always observed my birthday on the date of my choosing, and my friends and family do the same. Well, I know that the whole thing can sound a little silly, but now I always feel great on my birthday. Making that choice really did prove a turning point in my life. I don't mean for anyone to do precisely the same thing. Just the same you can choose to make this very moment a turning point in your own life.

Both the childhood *Game*—R10—and the *Milestone*—R34—reflect the personal qualities that underlie one's capacity to make a useful contribution. So contemplate how best to use those same gifts to realize a future milestone. Never let a previous milestone limit current aspirations. It may be that prior milestone reflected another person's values anyway. Now is a good time to choose a future milestone of your own.

The *Game*—R10, *Disposition*—R1, *Talisman*—R26, and *Gift*—R2 all reflect the special talents we bring. Cogitato's task is to figure a way to turn them into contributions, and then bring them to market.

Take a long, hard look at your *Calling*—R36—and your *Dream*—

R39. If they are genuinely unrealistic, then scrap them both right now, for they can only result in frustration and heartache. But if they are realistic, and if you really can pursue these aspirations—at least on a part time basis—then honestly, what is holding you back?

The *Wish*—R38—is often nothing more than the hope of a quick fix. In the real world prompt panaceas are few and far between, so either discard the wish, or apply some wishcraft. The requisite ingredients—creativity, focus, and hard work—are all readily available, and if you need a helping hand, then as my father used to say, look no further than the end of your arm.

Let's look at some actual responses to the Wareham CLIQ and you'll quickly see how everything works.

DAMON SMALL

Damon	Q#	24, prison inmate, small-time dealer and user
Turning Point	13	The defining moment of my life was to discover that my father is a killer.
Game	10	As a child I loved to hang around the streets.
Milestone	34	My most significant achievement is still to be alive.
Disposition	1	I am very nice with people, but they take advantage of me.
Talisman	26	The thing I like about myself is my survival skills.
Gift	2	My greatest talent won't succeed.
Calling	36	If I could have any career I'd be a porn star because I like to have sex with women for money.
Dream	39	My dream is to get somewhere in life.
Wish	38	I wish I could be on the streets instead of in jail.

Yes, that's the very same Damon we discussed earlier. He's an engaging enough fellow, so I can appreciate how he talked his way into my class. The milestone itself, survival, is neutral. The turning point, discovering that his father is a murderer, might one day prove positive, but for the foreseeable future it is likely to remain negative. Damon both discounts and undermines the value of his talisman by focusing upon mere survival. The aspiration to "get somewhere" in life is hazy at best. The hankering to be a porno star, as we've already seen, probably reflects the emotional wounds that lack of love and affection has afflicted. Damon's need to attract attention with this dubious calling is also simply one more way to sound the bugle and advance to the rear—or wherever. His wish—R38—to return to his absorbing game—R10—in the relative happiness of the streets will all too soon come true. That he will find freedom there, however, is in no way a sure bet.

WILLIAM QUAVER

William	Q#	39, laborer, convicted of petty theft, drug possession
Turning Point	13	The defining moment of my life was to get arrested again.
Game	10	As a child I loved to play basketball, swim, play the drums, and work.
Milestone	34	My most significant achievement was staying drug-free for three years.
Disposition	1	I am very willing to do whatever it takes to live right.
Talisman	36	The thing I like about myself is that I'm easygoing and do what I got to.
Gift	2	My greatest talent is that God gave me a beautiful wife and three wonderful sons.
Calling	36	If I could have any career I—doesn't matter, because I need to be normal, not rich.

Dream	39	My dream is to get back with my wife and kids, be responsible, stay away from drugs, and have a good job.
Wish	38	I wish my wife would come and see me, and that we could get back together some day.

William's dream of family, employment, and personal responsibility seems okay—maybe. Unfortunately, though a willing worker, an Obedio actually, William's progress is impeded by limited skills and the need for a leader to drive him. The reference to drugs is subtly negative. In saying that he merely dreams of staying away from drugs, he is actually giving those opiates a chance to step back into his life. His wife might well be staying away from William for that very reason. William dismisses the idea of a vocation by asserting that he wants to be "normal, not rich." In fact, the odds of living that normal life and making good on all his dreams would dramatically improve if he can discover passion for a specific vocation.

VINCENT VICTOR

Vincent	Q#	42, Entrepreneur
Turning Point	13	The defining moment of my life was to discover that I could make whatever I wanted of myself.
Game	10	As a child I loved to read biographies and play football.
Milestone	34	My most significant achievement was to be made partner in a major law firm at age twenty-seven.
Disposition	1	I am very anxious to optimize my talents.
Talisman	26	The thing I like about myself is my focus.
Gift	2	My greatest talent is my ability to make other people rich.

Calling	36	If I could have any career I'd be an entrepreneur.
Dream	39	My dream is to create a major international resort.
Wish	38	I wish for nothing for myself.

As the son of a minority blue-collar worker, Vincent paid his own way through college, attending part-time. He was recruited directly into a prestigious legal firm, but after being made partner faster than anyone in the firm, he quit to become a business executive. In just two years he was tapped to lead a major organization, which he handled with great aplomb and success. At that point, however, he sought my advice and confided that running a large organization wasn't making him as happy as he had hoped. Following that series of consultations, Vincent quit his big-time CEO role, started his own investment firm—and now counts his net worth in the hundreds of millions of dollars. Pretty good, right? In terms of the CLIQ, Vincent's current dream accords with his talents, his childhood pursuits, and his ultimate focus on making a contribution to others has repaid him handsomely. There's a lesson in that profile for everyone.

CHAPTER 10

Cogitato's Message
In a Nutshell

We must live as we think,
            otherwise we shall end up thinking as we have lived.

—Paul Bourget

To waken—to truly waken—is to transform the iron ball of unrealism into the first of three circles of success—an Integrated Value System.

The value system is the prism through which we view the world. All our perceptions pass through it and all our thoughts are colored by it. An enlightened person is someone whose values—the constellation of beliefs that filters his perceptions—are integrated with reality. Then, if he acts in accordance with his beliefs, he is also acting in harmony with the world, and therefore likely to choose his own best interests and achieve his goals.

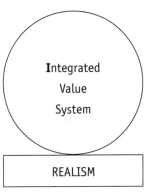

So let's just take that first circle and toss it into the air as a conjurer might—like so—

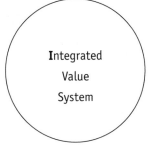

then bring it back down and split it into three circles, like so—

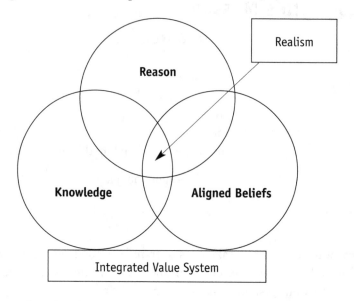

In this set of circles, knowledge, reason, and aligned beliefs create an inner overlap at the center of the three circles. We can call the diagram itself an Integrated Value System, and the overlap Realism.

So, then, the way out of prison, for both the prison inmate and corporate inmate, begins with the resolution to gain control of one's own thinking, and develop values and aspirations that align with reality—and the first step in this direction is to dispel the mistaken, imprisoning, carryover beliefs—illusions, actually—that essentially spring from childhood dependency.

PART THREE

Enlist Advancio

The Warrior Within Will Win the Day

When the time for thinking is past, and the moment for action at hand, Advancio—the warrior within—emerges from his resting place in the center of your chest, assumes control of your physicality, and strides into the arena of the world to get the job done. Former United States President Teddy Roosevelt lauded Advancio's duty along with his skills, in a rousing speech to the Sorbonne: "It is not the critic who counts, not the man who points out how the strong man stumbled, or where the doer of deeds could have done better. The credit belongs to the man who is actually in the arena; whose face is marred by the dust and sweat and blood; who strives valiantly; who errs and comes short again and again; who knows the great enthusiasms, the great devotions and spends himself in a worthy course; who at the best, knows in the end the triumph of high achievement, and who, at worst, if he fails, at least fails while daring greatly; so that his place shall never be with those cold and timid souls who know neither victory nor defeat."

CHAPTER 11

MAGIC CIRCLE NUMBER 2
The In-the-Moment Grappling Style
& How to Race a Motorcycle

To set the cause above renown,
To love the game beyond the prize
To honor while you strike him down
The foe that comes with fearless eyes.

—Sir Henry Newbolt

"I used to own a motorcycle, too," says Herbert. He's taut, thickset, and a great debater. "It was a 750cc racer. And I *really* raced it, too."

"But I guess you can't race it around Rikers," I joke.

"Well, no—it threw me off at 85 miles an hour."

His face is scarred. "You look okay. Did they salvage the bike?"

"Well, yes. They fixed it up. But then six months later I got back on and raced it again." He smiles wanly. "*That* was when I wrote it off." He drops his voice. "And almost killed myself as well."

Life, like motorcycle racing, calls for survival skills and a clear comprehension of physical laws. I ride a motorcycle, too, which is how that whole conversation got going, so I know that the ability to take a corner is governed by the physical laws of gravity and motion, which dictate that if I go too fast I'll lose control and fall off. If I hone my skills, however, I can stay on the bike and take the corner at increasingly higher speeds. Ultimately, of course, there's a speed beyond which *anyone*, no matter how skilled, will be thrown from the vehicle.

Whether I suffer serious injury is still in my own hands, however. If I'm wearing shorts and a tee shirt I'll hit the road and suffer serious injuries. If I've invested in leather outerwear and a crash helmet the road won't hurt me nearly so much and I'll probably survive to ride again. The point, of course, is that within the framework of physical law, each rider creates his own unique reality.

165

And so it is in the ride through life. But the laws of life are not merely physical, they're also emotional, social, and legal. If I ride through life carelessly my leather armor may protect me from physical harm in the event of an accident. If I harm others in the process, however, I'll feel rotten—unless I'm a sociopath—and likely lose friends, too. Feelings of shame and guilt are therefore akin to prison sentences meted out by oneself and society. Assume, for one moment, that I rode my motorcycle at 100 miles per hour under the influence of alcohol, suffered a nasty accident, broke a few limbs, killed a stranger, and received a prison sentence. In the confines of my prison cell, I could choose to blame the buddy who tempted me to drink. Or I could blame the other vehicle—or my own brakes, or the traffic, or a vindictive prosecutor, or an unfeeling judge. Or maybe I could contemplate my own unrealism and irresponsibility.

The point is that *we create our own reality.*

So if the world is not to our liking, we can change it. George Bernard Shaw observed that all progress depends upon the unreasonable man, for the reasonable man accepts things the way they are. A real leader sees something that doesn't exist, persuades others to see it too—and then works to make it a reality.

A competent leader is both imaginative and practical. He knows that he cannot plant his feet in the air. He knows that to change the world he must proceed from a sound understanding of how things actually work, and then go on to use those very same rules to make changes.

So now, having dreamed of building a castle in the air, let's enlist Advancio to commence the task of building that edifice from the foundation up, one brick at a time.

The key to his effectiveness will lie in his warrior way of wrestling with the world in order to get what he wants or needs—his *grappling style.* So what is the *best* style? Well, at least part of the answer to that question lies in the case of the unsung juggler.

The Case of the Unsung Juggler

Charlie Chaplin, in his delightful autobiography, tells a story from his circus days of a brilliant juggler, lamenting that his finest-ever feat was failing to attract the level of applause that it deserved. Hoping to help, the circus owner observed the utterly brilliant achievement, then offered some advice. "You're making it look too easy, you don't sell it. You should miss it several times, then do it." The juggler paused and shrugged. "I am not expert enough to miss it yet," he replied.

The elegant successes of an outstanding performer can seem deceptively easy. There are at least a couple of reasons for this. First, success usually entails getting a lot of things right. The failure of one component can sabotage everything. Second, to be successful an executive must possess many qualities—whereas the absence of merely one of them will likely render him mediocre at best.

Much the same might be said of an ex-offender departing the prison gate. One impulsive action can ruin an entire life. And without confidence in his ability to make a real contribution in the outside world, he'll likely fall into the kind of mediocre life that inevitably leads to frustration, psychic analgesics, and enforced rehabilitation.

In fact, the most successful warriors are pragmatists who instinctively adjust their grappling styles to the situation and the moment at hand. I call this an *In-the-Moment* grappling style.

Escaping the Prison of Obedience

The trouble with the mediocre performer is that he's stuck with an obsolete grappling style. His machinations used to work, but now they don't. That's because the world has changed and he hasn't. His maneuvers are geared to a past era, not to the here and now and the situation at hand.

The first thing to consider, then, is the extent to which your warrior within might still be trapped within the prison of obedience. This is typically revealed in the Wareham CLIQ by comparing the relationship between the Prime Parental Injunction and the related elements of Compliance, Rivalry, and Self-Rating. You might like to list your own responses below.

The Prison of Obedience	Q#	Sentence Stem
Prime Parental Injunction (PPIN)	4	My parents always told me I should

Compliance	7	Obeying my father
Rivalry	28	When a peer does better I
Rating	31	Compared with others, I

Now, let's see how the responses of real-life executives compare with the responses of prison inmates.

➤ Paradoxically, the typical prime parental injunction—the *PPIN*, R4—of both executives and prison inmates was to behave well, get a good education, and become professionals. Reactions to masculine authority—*Compliance*, R7—revealed that nine out of ten executives learned to get along with authority. In half of those homes, absolute compliance was effectively the law. In the other half, it was acceded to affectionately as the sensible route. Entrepreneurs—as opposed to executives—fall into the Contrarian 10 percent reporting problems with authority.*

➤ When outshone by a peer—see *Rivalry*, R28—four of five executives congratulate that peer, while one out of five feel piqued. By comparison, two of three prisoners congratulate the peer who excels, and one out of three feels diminished or competitive. The quick moral seems to be that successful people gradually outgrow sibling rivalry. They focus upon the task at hand and are less inclined to be in competition with childhood ghosts.

➤ The *Rating*—R31—is even more interesting. All executives rated themselves positively. Only 45 percent of prisoners did the same. Moreover, the prisoners who rated themselves positively often described themselves as "special." Pretty clearly, they wanted to claim the status of the preferred and special child.

---

*Sigmund Freud's theory is that entrepreneurs hate their fathers and want to bed their mothers. The entrepreneur deals with this predicament by incorporating himself. The corporation then effectively becomes both lover and mother, and the father is forbidden to set foot inside the door.

A look over your own responses may reveal Contrario or Obedio tendencies, but hold that thought in your head as we turn to analyzing some of the other key elements of your grappling style.

KEY ELEMENTS OF THE GRAPPLING STYLE

The Wareham CLIQ measures several key elements of your grappling style. These include the primary ingrained technique or Grappler; the favored method for influencing others, or Mind-Changer; the preferred strategy for overcoming obstacles, or Implement; the counterproductive behavior that sabotages your efforts, or Tripwire; and the tool that's missing from your methodology, or Missing Part. List your own responses below:

Grappling Style	Q#	Sentence Stem
Grappler	22	My way of winning the struggle to get what I want is to
Mind-Changer	23	I persuaded him to change his mind by
Implement	16	If I can't get what I want, I
Tripwire	27	What gets me into trouble is
Missing Part	29	If I would only

For a whopping 41 percent of executives, the *Grappler*—R22—is "a plan." For 24 percent the grappler is "team effort and leadership." Another 21 percent cite "delegation"—with the savviest executives adding "to the right person." The final 14 percent of executives say that they jump in and "just do it."

Prisoners show entirely different response clusters. None of them are thinking about teams or delegation, which is understandable, of course. Only 10 percent cite planning as a grappler, though a further 13 percent cite the use of intellect or imagination. Most, 43 percent, cite perseverance and greater effort. Seventeen percent rely upon either God or a positive attitude. Nine percent cite "whatever it takes." And 6 percent failed to respond at all, which might be a grappler all of its own.

One lesson is that executives, being better educated, are more apt to think in terms of an overall context and then go on to customize specific solutions for specific problems. Prisoners, on the other hand, seldom step back and think in terms of the big picture. Instead they merely apply hard work and perseverance to the immediate problem. It may be politically incorrect to say but this kind of ingrained blinkered thinking reflects a legacy of enslavement, under the yoke of which, following orders was vital, and thinking was severely punished. Whatever the moral, however, effort is infinitely more effective when applied within the framework of a viable, adjustable plan.

The *Mind-Changer*—R23—is a key element in the grappling style. More than half (52 percent) of all executives cite reason or logic as their mind-changer. Discussion (13 percent) and weighing of the options (11 percent) come next. Pointing out the downside collects 6 percent. The savviest of the savvy executives, 12 percent, say, "by appealing to his self-interest."

Logic as a mind-changer accounts for only 10 percent of prisoners. One fifth cite general discussion. A further 30 percent like to cite concrete illustrations from their own lives. Five percent focus on the downside. Weighing the options accounts for 12 percent. Ten percent cite manipulation or the capacity to wring out "pity." Five percent of prison inmates—less than half that of executives—say, "by appealing to his self-interest."

We reach for the *Implement*—R16—when we run out of other options. Only one executive in ten says that he accepts the setback. More than half of all executives, complete this stem by saying, effectively, "I get it *somehow*." An additional, wily 36 percent say that they change their tactics in order to get what they want. Overall, nine out of ten executives refuse to take no for an answer.

By contrast, 40 percent of prisoners say that they accept the setback. One in four gets angry. One in ten suffers feelings of disappointment. Overall, only one in four prisoners attempts to overcome the obstacle before him. One way or another, nearly four of five prisoners find a way to sound the bugle and advance to the rear!

The *Tripwire*—R27—often reflects the tip of the kind of iceberg that sunk the Titanic. For nearly 30 percent of executives the tripwire is being "too honest," or "too outspoken"—or otherwise unable to tame the tongue. One in five cites impatience. One in five cites inability to stick to priorities, poor time management, or general overload. And a further one in ten cites perfectionism.

Nearly 30 percent of prisoners have problems with being "too honest," but call it what it is—"bad attitude," "stubbornness," and "arrogance." Mixing with the wrong people and drug addiction account for one quarter of prisoners, and "self-deception" accounts for another quarter.

If the *Missing Part*—R29—were present the tripwire might not come into play. For example, 44 percent of all executives say something like, "If only there were more hours in my day," yet these are typically the same people who say, "What gets me into trouble is my perfectionism" or "I take on more work than I can handle." Or consider that faulty people skills account for a further 28 percent of executive missing parts, so "If only I would keep my big mouth shut" is thus coupled with "What gets me into trouble is that I tell it like it is."

Prisoners, of course, are infinitely less concerned with not having enough hours in the day. Their major concern is how to handle release. They mostly say, "If I would only find a job when I get out of here," without grasping how this relates to the often-cited missing part, "What gets me into trouble is my attitude."

Now, then, let's once again compare your responses with those of executives—both effective and ineffective—and prison inmates.

WAYNE SPARKLESS

Wayne	Q#	45, former franchise operator
Grappler	22	My way of winning the struggle is to ease myself into control of the process.
Mind-Changer	23	I persuaded him to change his mind by making him think it was his idea.
Implement	16	If I can't get what I want my stomach plays up.
Tripwire	27	What gets me into trouble is promising too much.

Missing Part	29	If I would only have someone refer me another big-ticket client to get out of my current situation.

You remember Wayne. He's the fellow who cheated his business partner and lost his franchise. Wayne's grappler and mind-changer both reflect a penchant for deviousness. More intriguingly, this particular implement, dyspepsia, is actually an impediment that likely springs from the pressure of the falling behind in his accounting, and the knowledge that he is masking a guilty secret. The tripwire, promising too much, is clearly related to the missing part, the hunt for someone to pay the bills. Taken together, the pattern in this grappling style seems a sure-fire cluster of failing tussles—which is how it all turned out.

MICKEY DODGE

Mickey	Q#	30, illegal dealer of controlled substances
Grappler	22	My way of winning the struggle is to apply myself forcefully.
Mind-Changer	23	I persuaded him to change his mind by staring him down.
Implement	16	If I can't get what I want people should be careful.
Tripwire	27	What gets me into trouble is trying to live at the level of a drug dealer.
Missing Part	29	If I would only find a way to earn a big income without resorting to crime.

Thirty-year-old Mickey Dodge is a troubled fellow. The grappler, mind-changer, and implement all suggest an underlying penchant for violence. Like Wayne, he's caught in the monkey trap of not being able to let go of the very lifestyle that effectively imprisons him. His tripwire, the wish to live in the style of drug dealer, is common enough in

Mickey's milieu, and therefore doubly tempting. The missing part matches Wayne's: the very same inability to earn an income within an ethical framework. Compare these two rather depressing cases with the dynamic leader of a major business unit.

BARRY BOUNDLESS

Barry	Q#	48, business unit leader
Grappler	22	My way of winning the struggle is to help my team develop a plan, set priorities, then run like the wind itself, with me leading the charge.
Mind-Changer	23	I persuaded him to change his mind by negotiating a win-win deal.
Implement	16	If I can't get what I want I reframe the problem, then go back and sell the solution.
Tripwire	27	What gets me into trouble is my impatience to show results.
Missing Part	29	If I would only learn to balance time.

Barry is an inspiration to his staff, but his wife says he works too hard and she's probably right. Business is an obsession for Barry. The grappler reflects an ingrained habit of seeing his role through his subordinates' eyes. He wants to be both coach and leader. The mind-changer shows an immediate and specific understanding of the win-win concept. The implement, a combination of imagination and perseverance, shows a similar concern. The tripwire and the missing part both relate to time-management issues, but all things considered, Barry has mastered Rudyard Kipling's injunction to "fill the unforgiving minute with sixty seconds' worth of distance run." Well, that's what his boss says, anyway.

Now that you've compared some grappling styles to your own, you might want to think about building and enhancing an *In-the-Moment* style. One way to do this is to incorporate some of the powerful implements favored by outstanding performers.

THE UNSHAKABLE KNACK

Skill is more than talent. A person with much talent can perform a certain procedure naturally. He doesn't need to work as hard to hone his skill as a person of lesser talent. Yet time and again, it's the person of lesser talent driven by inner demons to overcome his shortcomings who works his way to the top. He transforms himself into a winner by applying what I call the three Ps: procedure, practice, and perseverance.

Procedure can involve anything from the striking of a ball to the management of a difficult employee. The trick is to break the task into a series of fundamental procedures and master each. This means developing an ingrained, repeatable grappling style. The key element in such a style is a sense of effortless grace—but of course that grace is seldom as effortless as it seems.

Practice is what we do to hone the procedure and ingrain the grappling style. That's why the ambitious golfer dedicates himself to "grooving his swing." Practice separates the pro from the dilettante. The key to practice is to keep the outcome in mind, and to set those milestones we spoke of earlier. It's easier to practice when we know we're making progress toward a goal.

Perseverance is the simple capacity to keep on going—and going, and going. Former United States President Calvin Coolidge observed, "Nothing in the world can take the place of perseverance. Talent will not: nothing is more common than unsuccessful men with talent. Genius will not: unrewarded genius is almost a proverb. Education will not: the world is full of educated derelicts. Perseverance and determination alone are omnipotent. The slogan, press on, has solved and always will solve the problems of the human race."

THE DECOMPRESSOR

Wouldn't it be nice to discover that there's some secret confidence builder that champions use to ease pressure situations?

In fact, after acquiring a repeatable skill—or unshakable knack—the difference between the champion and the runner-up comes down to luck and the ability to manage one's emotions under pressure.

Some people simply perform better under pressure than others, of course. Paradoxically, the best way to outfox such people is to *forget* about winning. Instead we should aim merely to produce our personal best—and, in the heat of battle, the best way to achieve that lies in three words: *composure, focus, and trust.*

➤ Composure is a matter of centering oneself. It's a matter of closing out the world for a moment or two, taking a half-dozen deep breaths, then formulating and holding the image of an effortless, graceful execution.

➤ By focus I mean short-term focus—putting the overall outcome out of mind and concentrating entirely on each moment. Letting the mind drift to contemplate victory or defeat is the path to an unhappy outcome. Remain in the moment and focus upon performance in the here and now.

➤ To trust means not to attempt to second-guess one's immediate actions. To trust completely is to act as if it were impossible to fail. It is a matter of letting go of conscious control and letting the unconscious take over. Gus D'Amato, the famous boxing coach, had a lovely piece of advice along these lines. As the opening bell sounded, he'd lean into his fighter's ear and say, "It's just fifteen rounds of hard sparring—and you're in charge!" He knew that the fighter had a better chance of winning by trusting his skills than fretting about the outcome. George Balanchine, the dancer, described the same kind of letting go: "On Monday, I practice. On Tuesday, I practice. On Wednesday, I practice. On Thursday, I practice. But on Friday and Saturday, I forget about all my practicing, and I *dance!*"

THE SCISSORS

Elbert Hubbard in his classic essay, "A Message to Garcia," writes memorably about what I call the scissors:

In all this Cuban business there is one man that stands out on the horizon of my memory like Mars at perihelion. When war broke out between Spain and the United States, it was very necessary to communicate quickly with the leader of the Insurgents. Garcia was somewhere in the mountain vastnesses of Cuba—no one knew where. No mail or telegraph could reach him. The President must secure his co-operation, and quickly. What to do! Someone said to the President, "There's a fellow by the name of Rowan who will find Garcia for you, if anybody can."

Rowan was sent for and given a letter to be delivered to Garcia. How "the fellow by the name of Rowan" took the letter, sealed it up in an oil-skin pouch, strapped it over his heart, in four days landed by night off the coast of Cuba from an open boat, disappeared into the jungle, and in three weeks came out on the other side of the island, having traversed a hostile country on foot, and having delivered his letter to Garcia, are things I have no special desire now to tell in detail. The point I wish to make is this: McKinley gave Rowan a letter to be delivered to Garcia; Rowan took the letter and did not ask, "Where is he at?" By the Eternal! There is a man whose form should be cast in deathless bronze and the statue placed in every college in the land. It is not book-learning young men need, nor instruction about this or that, but a stiffening of the vertebrae which will cause them to be loyal to a trust, to act promptly, concentrate their energies; do the thing—"carry a message to Garcia!"

The two blades of any dedicated messenger's scissors are initiative and perseverance. The first blade, initiative, is the capacity to see the right thing, to find the most effective way to get it done, and then to *do it*— all without having to be told. We looked briefly at that second blade of perseverance, but there's more to say.

Perseverance involves an underlying process. We don't seem to be getting anywhere. We feel like giving up but we press on. Still nothing seems to happen. But in fact our perseverance is tapping the unconscious mind. The next time we come to practice we find that the mind has somehow put our practice to good use. Now, mastering the procedure is easier. Suddenly, all our practice lifts us to a higher plateau of performance. We're suddenly surprised to find that the procedure we'd been struggling to instill from the outside now seems to be coming from inside of us.

We also need to bear in mind, however, that mere persistence with an obsolete grappling style will likely prove futile—or even counter-productive. The following diagram makes the point.

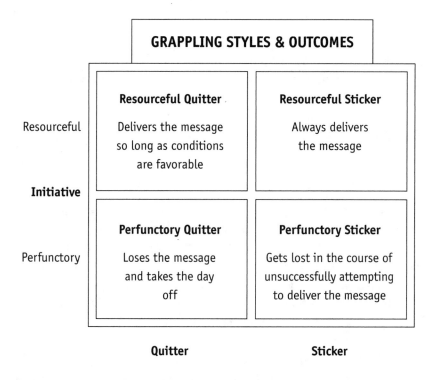

GRAPPLING STYLES & OUTCOMES

	Quitter	**Sticker**
Resourceful	**Resourceful Quitter** Delivers the message so long as conditions are favorable	**Resourceful Sticker** Always delivers the message
Perfunctory	**Perfunctory Quitter** Loses the message and takes the day off	**Perfunctory Sticker** Gets lost in the course of unsuccessfully attempting to deliver the message

Initiative

PERSEVERANCE

Great executives fit into the upper-right resourceful-sticker quadrant. Average executives—some of whom are highly celebrated—fit into the upper left, resourceful-quitter quadrant. All kinds of inmates, corporate and actual, are imprisoned within the bottom two quadrants, but could escape if only they could think of creating new grappling styles.

PARETO'S ARC

Pareto was the fellow who discovered what we now call the "eighty-twenty rule." He showed, statistically, that an eighty-twenty relationship is generally to be discovered between cause and effect.

Thus:

> ➤ 20 percent of the salespeople produce 80 percent of the income—so recruit with care and don't fret over the termination of an incompetent.

> ➤ 80 percent of the customer complaints spring from just 20 percent of the production or distribution problems—so focus on fixing the most vital underlying problems instead of merely running around "putting out fires."

> ➤ 20 percent of the reading public reads 80 percent of the books—so if you're a publisher, you need to know that a book pitched to non-readers is likely to fail.

When I explain the eighty-twenty rule at Rikers I make two points. First, that the rule can be applied to just about every aspect of life, so we should identify and rid ourselves of the 20 percent of the issues that are causing 80 percent of our problems. Second, I point out that 80 percent of classroom aggravation is caused by 20 percent of the pupils. Then I ask the class a question. "How do you think I should deal with the 20 percent who feel compelled to act out?"

"Toss them out?" comes the reply.

"Well, no—I don't like to do that. I figure that they're in prison—and in my class—precisely because acting out is a key problem that so far they've not been able to bring under control. I also assume that it's my duty to make them aware of that fact, and then go help them to quit that very same self-defeating behavior."

"Hey, teach—way to go!"

"Yeah, well, that's the good news. The bad news, for some, is that I also apply the three-strikes-and-you're-out rule. You all know what that is, right?" There's a murmuring and nodding of heads. "I apply *that* rule because my ultimate responsibility is to the 80 percent who want to learn, not the 20 percent who don't. So, now, does everybody understand the eighty-twenty rule?"

In fact, inmates can be quicker to appreciate the beauty of the eighty-twenty rule than some bureaucrats. One misguided program administrator got the rule all upside down and restricted class recruitment to the 80 percent of inmates *least* capable of learning—then couldn't figure out why just about everything went haywire!

THE PRIORITY BOX

The Priority Box, another implement favored by *In-the-Moment* grapplers, is tremendously effective in helping accomplish long-term goals. They simply plot their problems and goals in terms of Importance and Urgency.

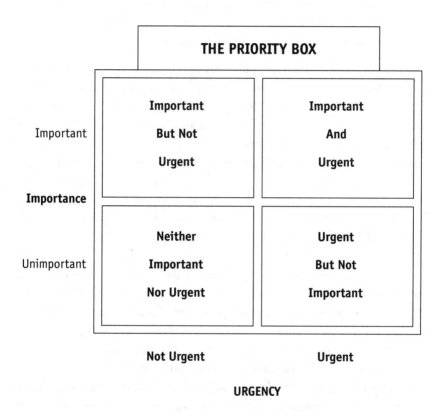

Let's consider what we might be able to learn from Rafael. He's just been released from Rikers and he's riding the train back into the city. Most of the tasks that face him are both urgent and important, but for the purpose of setting priorities he's thinking along the following lines:

- *Urgent and important.* Contact the parole officer. Find somewhere to live. A halfway house would ease a lot of problems. Get some walking-around money. Find some job leads.

- *Urgent but not important.* Renew soon-to-expire driving license. Attend to appearances. Assemble an interview wardrobe.

- *Neither important nor urgent.* Take in a movie. Build a new CD collection. Visit some of the old gang.

- *Important but not urgent.* Create a new love relationship. Improve basic skills. Get some better credentials. Get a career going. Write some poems and think about joining a poetry slam group.

All of the urgent tasks are commanding Rafael's immediate attention, of course. He's thinking that he'll head straight to the parole office. Maybe they'll know of a halfway house. They might even have a job suggestion. Tomorrow he'll set about renewing the driving license and sprucing himself up. The movie and the CD collection are neither urgent nor important, so he'll get on to them sometime down the road. And since he's thinking so clearly, maybe never will be soon enough to reconnect with anyone from the old gang. It would be nice to heat up a piece of love relationship, but that's going to have to go onto the back burner with all that other long-term stuff.

"But hang on there a moment, Rafael." That very clear and adult voice belongs to Cogitato. He's seized momentary control from Advancio. "If you're really serious about breaking out of prison, go back and take a long hard look at those important-but-not-urgent items—the credentials, the career, and the poetry. Sure, for this week they can wait. But even then don't put them *completely* out of mind. These big issues are key to long-term breakout. The paradox is that even though they can wait, they'll nonetheless start to alter the course and quality of your life in the very moment you start to seriously address them. So don't just leave them to go stale. Bring them onto the front burner by:

- Breaking them into a series of milestones.

- Inserting the various tasks that will lead to those milestones into the important and urgent quadrant.

➤ Scheduling those tasks in your calendar.

➤ Attacking at least one of these tasks at the beginning of each day.

➤ Dedicating at least an hour of every day to the important and urgent quadrant.

Cogitato's right. I know that from personal experience. I was surprised, for example, when my publisher recently reminded me that I've written eight books. In fact, without the spur of a deadline I doubt I'd ever have written anything. Much the same is true for everything I've ever accomplished. The key to getting the big things out of the way has *always* been to have Cogitato figure out a series of goals, milestones, and deadlines, and then to trust Advancio to take care of everything else. As for me, well, I just sit back and watch.

CHAPTER 12

How to Talk Your Way Out of Trouble
& Into a Good Time

If I had kept my mouth shut I wouldn't be here.

—sign under a mounted fish

"Please let me out of jail. I dealt a little cocaine, but if I didn't somebody else would have. What I did made no difference to anyone. My kids miss me and need me to come home. And I miss my girlfriend, too. I lie awake at night and dream of her. I'm not a threat to anyone. Not anymore. I've attended anger management classes and victim awareness classes. I have it under control now. This time, I'll be looking hard for a job. I'll really be trying."

Mark, who is almost thirty, has just completed an exercise in persuasive speaking. Each inmate makes a one-minute plea for immediate release to an imaginary parole board. I have promised, with a wink, that the best speaker will be able to depart the prison with me when I leave. I give no clues as to what the imaginary parole board might be seeking. It is up to each speaker to make his best case.

I run this exercise very early in the semester, and the result rarely fails to astonish me. Only a tiny percentage of the class shows an appreciation of what it takes to persuade anyone of anything.

Mark's speech is, alas, typical of the offerings. At the completion of the exercise, I tell a story:

A man goes to the doctor. "I have bad news and good news for you," says the doctor. "The bad news is that you have terminal cancer and just six months to live." The patient is utterly disconsolate. "Whatever, then," he sobs, "could be the good news?" The doctor tosses a glance in the direction of a sultry young nurse. "You see that lovely young girl?" he says. The patient's eyes follow the doctor's glance. The nurse in question is indeed a vision of youthful loveliness. "Well, the good news," says the doctor, smiling broadly, "is that I'm engaged in a deliciously wild and torrid affair with her."

I wait for the laughter to subside,, then extract the moral. "That doctor has a problem," I say. "He's too self-involved to give his patient proper treatment. Unfortunately, we saw that same brand of self-involvement during the course of your pleas to the parole board. You see everything from your own point of view. You're so absorbed in the idea of getting home and getting laid that you fail to see the need to treat the cancer in your own lives. We're talking about an exercise in the art of *persuasion*. Just about every last one of you made the same mistake. You told of your pain, and you tried to shift the blame, or to minimize it. Will *that* persuade a parole board to set you free? Of course not! The key to persuasion is not to attempt to inspire pity. The key is to appeal to the self-interest of the parole board. And what they want is for you to convince them that if they set you free, then that decision will make *them* look good. They also want to hear that you'll make their lives easier by becoming a taxpayer. They want to hear that you've changed. They want you to spell out that you're ready to become part of the solution, not the same old part of the same old problem. So, in the end, it boils down to the five Rs: Responsibility, Remorse, Reorientation, Rehabilitation, and Readiness to go out into the world and make a contribution."

"I got busted for drugs," interjects Kareem with a sly smile. "It's a victimless crime. Should *I* feel remorse?"

I pause. "Do your parents think that getting high is a victimless crime, Kareem?"

"I never asked them."

I pluck a sheet of paper from my vest pocket. "Of course you didn't. So let me share a poem that might make us all wonder about both victimless crime and remorse. It's very a sensitive piece, so make a special effort to savor the delicacy of the language. It's called 'Parental Love in the Twenty-First Century,' and it goes like this—"

> *I vomited you out of my house*
> *Like a putrid smelly mouse,*
> *Like a fermented maggot . . . scum!*
> *You are a dog! You are a bum!*
> *You are sneaky and you are dumb!*

I sight some smiles and hear some chuckles—

> *You drove me to insanity.*
> *You drove me to senility.*
> *You drove me to sterility.*
> *You pierced my brain with a thousand thumbtack nails.*
> *You squeezed, in the vice of your duplicity, my entrails.*
> *I should have drowned you in my tub.*
> *I should have fed you rat poison,*
> *My son: the rat!*

The entire class is suddenly paying rapt attention—

> *You stole from me, insulted me, betrayed me,*
> *Made my bankbooks and my furniture disappear,*
> *Got your pals to stab me in the rear,*
> *While hiding little bags of white powder,*
> *Inside your mattress and in your underwear,*
> *And in pockets inside your sleeve*
> *To make me grieve.*

Kareem's gaze is steadfastly to the floor—

> *You really took me for a ride,*
> *A ride I can't describe,*
> *Full of sorrow and of pain*
> *Suffered in vain.*
> *I took your temper, I took your screams,*
> *Forgot my prayers, forgot my dreams,*
> *Waiting in silence with hope ajar,*
> *Looking wistfully to the stars*
> *For my salvation*
> *Which never came . . .*

I take a long, deep breath. The silence is palpable—

> *If you come back, I swear,*
> *I'll grab my handgun,*
> *I'll close the shutters,*
> *And as soon as you open the door*
> *Bang! Bang! No more!*
> *I'll shoot all my bullets*
> *Into your cockroach of a brain*
> *As empty as a tin cup.*

Now, the mocking conclusion—

> *I'm proud to be your father.*
> *I'm thrilled, I'm blessed*
> *To have a modern son*
> *Who will try to dispatch me quickly*
> *To get hold of all my money.*
> *Drop dead, Son!**

Gasps rend the air. Berry leads the chorus. "Hey! Hey! Hey!" he cries. "That dude is *angry!*"

"You'd be angry too!" says Johnson. "That kid put him through hell."

They all chime in, except for Kareem.

I pause for silence, then drop the big question. "So, do we really think that doing drugs is a victimless crime?"

All eyes turn to Kareem, but he's not in a mood to respond.

Dwayne, the gentle forty-year-old giant, steps into the silence. "Doing drugs never was and never will be a victimless crime." He directs his remarks to the class. "We've mostly all been down that road"—his voice is reproachful—"and those of us who knows our ass from our elbow, if you'll pardon my French, well, we know that that kid fucked up big-time, and that little asshole should feel ashamed of hisself." He turns back to me. "That's what remorse means, right?" Right.

At the end of the session I point out that Hector delivered the best plea. His command of English was shaky, but this is what he said:

> Ladies and Gentlemen of the parole board, I want to say immediately that I committed the crime—car theft—of which I was convicted and incarcerated, and that my behavior was inexcusable. I'm truly sorry that I committed the crime. I've expressed my sorrow and shame to the victim. I've also made complete restitution. Here in prison I've completed my General Educational Diploma. And in this program, I've acquired skills that have permitted me to get the offer of a secure job as soon as I get out. I am looking forward to returning home to my loving wife, and becoming a good father and, most importantly, a productive citizen. If you will release me, I will not let you down."

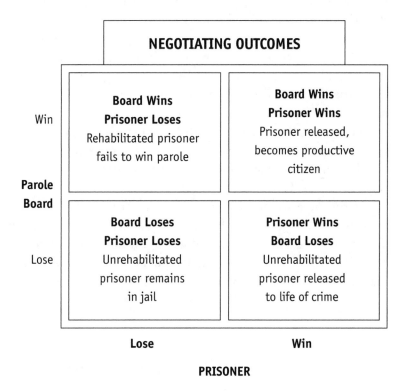

THE IN-THE-MOMENT MIND-CHANGER

You'd think by now that just about every person on earth would realize that the key to getting what you want in just about any kind of negotiation lies in the win-win concept of striking a deal whereby both parties get what they want. Consider, for example, the case of the two old ladies fighting over the only orange in a fruit shop. After a little discussion they discover that one wants the orange in order to squeeze the juice into a drink, whereas the other merely wants the rind for some icing to put on a cake. Armed with this knowledge, they both escape the same mental prison, and both become winners. We can apply this concept to the parole board illustration. It's a tad more complex, however, because both short-term and long-term considerations come into play.

In the lower-left quadrant everybody loses. The prisoner loses on two counts: he fails to see the light and he fails to win parole. The board loses on two counts: the reform system has failed to work and the prisoner remains a burden upon the state.

In the upper-left quadrant, the board wins—or at least does not entirely lose. It would be better for the board to have set the prisoner free, but at least they can't be blamed for making a mistake. The prisoner loses his bid for freedom, but can at least console himself with his new-found maturity.

In the lower-right quadrant, the prisoner wins release from incarceration, but remains in a mental prison and returns to a life of crime. The board, having mistakenly freed a menace to society, loses in every way.

In the upper-right quadrant, everybody is a winner. The rehabilitated prisoner is freed and becomes a productive tax-paying citizen. The members of the parole board win praise and satisfaction for their good judgment. They also optimize public funds so everybody ultimately winds up paying lower taxes. Well, that's the theory, anyway.

CHAPTER 13

Advancio's Message

In a Nutshell

Every sort of mastery is an increase of one's freedom.

—Henri Frederic Amiel

The Key to Advancio's success lies in transmuting the iron ball of an obsolete grappling style into the magic circle of an *In-the-Moment* grappling style—which looks something like this—

So let's just take that circle and toss it into the air as a conjurer might —like so—

189

then bring it back down and split it into three, like so—

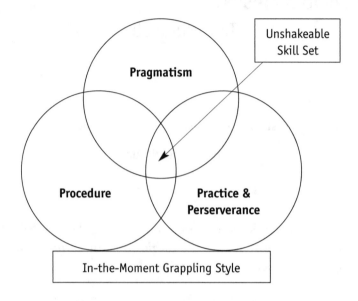

In this set of circles, Procedure, Practice, and Pragmatism create an inner overlap at the center. We can call the diagram itself an In-the-Moment Grappling Style, and the overlap an Unshakable Skill Set that we can apply, using the appropriate tools, to the demands of the situation and the moment.

The beauty of developing such a set of skills—and acquiring that range of tools—is that we simultaneously begin the transmutation process for the third and final imprisoning iron ball. But I'm getting ahead of myself, again.

PART FOUR

Embrace Nurturio

The Best Friend You Never Knew You Had

Nurturio is the friend you always wished for, the sibling you never knew, the parent you never had.

He regards you with unstinting affection and cheerfully overlooks your faults and foibles. His favorite line is from Blaise Pascal, "The heart has reasons that reason knows nothing of."

You feel better the moment Nurturio appears. His gift for saying the soothing thing brings out the best in you.

He holds your gifts equal to his own and always treats you as an equal. He always conveys a deep belief in your ability to handle your own problems.

You secretly worry that Nurturio doesn't comprehend your dark and undeserving side. In fact, however, he knows you better than you know yourself.

And, being the wizard that he is, Nurturio is always at the ready to work a little magic in your life—as he did in Rocky's.

CHAPTER 14

MAGIC CIRCLE NUMBER 3

The Intact Sense of Self-Esteem

& How to Step Out of a Wheelchair

In our personal lives when we find signs
        that we are speaking in our own accent, speaking our own minds,
        living by our own opinions,
we feel the pulse beat of our own personality coming to life again.

        —Irwin Edman

Rocky has a decided limp but carries himself proudly. He's slim, soft-spoken, intelligent, and insightful. He walks gingerly to the front of the class. "The most courageous thing I ever did," he says, "was to forgive the three so-called friends who out of mere personal animosity beat me unconscious and threw me from the top floor of a fifteen-story building." He leans forward on his slightly iffy left leg. "It happened twelve years ago when I was twenty-eight. I awoke in a hospital bed and stayed there for six months. Then I failed at three months of physical therapy. It was hell. The doctors said I'd never walk again and sent me home in a wheelchair."

"It took *courage* to forgive them?!" interjects José. "Maybe you've just got a self-esteem problem."

Rocky pauses and draws a deep breath. "I was sitting in that wheelchair and staring at my bedroom wall. I was tight with fury at the injustice of it all. I was also thinking that I really did want to walk again. So you know what I did? I prayed. And you know what? The answer flashed into my brain. *First you've gotta forgive those guys who threw you off the roof!* I've never been terribly religious but suddenly I decided that I really would forgive that bunch of cowards. And I did. And I sat

193

there in silence for several minutes. Forgiving them was easy, actually. The decision to get out of the wheelchair was much more difficult. A wheelchair can be a very comfortable place, you know. But, finally, I reached for my crutches and pulled myself out of the chair. Even with the crutches I could manage only three excruciatingly painful steps. But I knew it was a new beginning."

This counsel of forgiveness and acceptance is Nurturio's specialty. His voice is the voice of intuition. You've doubtless heard it in your own life. Sometimes, as a result of our not paying enough attention, it can seem weak, but most successful people tend to hear it clearly. Consider my friend Nadine, for example.

"As a young woman I had it made. I graduated Harvard University and Harvard Law School and stepped straight into a prestigious law firm. I had a top income and outstanding prospects. Everyone was so proud of me. I'd fulfilled all my parents' dreams. Yet I somehow felt incredibly empty. And then a voice inside of me urged me to do something I had never even contemplated—quit that job and take a lowly role with minimal income as a civil rights lawyer."

In consequence of heeding Nurturio, Nadine Strossen dedicated herself to her career and was ultimately appointed national president of the American Civil Liberties Union. "Looking back on that fateful decision, I disappointed many people," she says. "But the voice was insistent. It said that I had no choice. I would have to move on or effectively wither away." Ah, yes, the comfortable wheelchair. So many people fear to step out of it. Instead, they opt for a secure place in the hearts of others. They'll be taken care of. They'll just never know what it can be like to break free and run. Is it possible, really, to tell anyone how to break free of such a contraption? Well, yes, of course. Nurturio has some excellent advice. I know, because I made a conscious decision to listen for his advice in every prison class I ever ran. Time and again, I heard his voice. It often emanated from unlikely looking faces, but I always recognized its special quality. The inner cynic might prefer Nurturio to be a touch more hard-headed. Sometimes I felt like saying, Hey, Nurturio, we're talking to hardened criminals, not angels. I kept my silence, however. Then I went home and wrote down everything he said. Self-esteem was his strong suit. He seemed to know how to turn feelings of inferiority upside down.

How to Develop Authentic Feelings of Superiority

The primary elements of self-esteem are 1) a feeling of *adequacy* to handle the challenges of life; and 2) a sense of being *worthy* of success and therefore entitled to hold on to it. It can be helpful to chart these items into four quadrants:

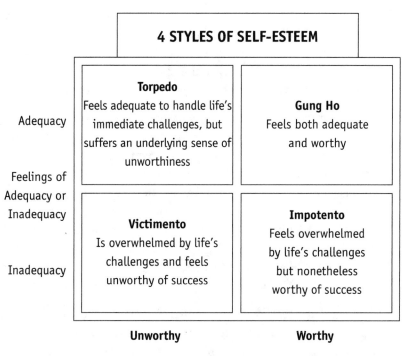

> ➤ **Gung Ho** in the Adequate/Worthy upper-right quadrant enjoys an intact sense of self-esteem. Gung Hos are generally comfortable overcoming obstacles, achieving success, and holding onto their winnings. The best executives generally come from this quadrant. If Gung Hos have a problem it might flow from being too well adjusted to need to demonstrate outstanding achievement.

> **Torpedoes** fit into the Adequate/Unworthy upper-left quadrant. Some are gifted, and some are merely corner-cutters. They're essentially competent to handle life's challenges and an underlying sense of unworthiness drives them to become overachievers. Unfortunately, their accomplishments merely exaggerate their feelings of shame. Success seems to have come too easily, leaving them feeling like impostors. Compliments therefore evoke guilt instead of satisfaction. In a desperate drive to overcome these feelings they strive for even greater successes. The result is the same but worse. Now they feel like even bigger phonies. In the end, Torpedoes turn their firepower upon themselves. They engage in unconscious acts of self-sabotage, with often quite spectacular results. I have met many such individuals, both in and out of my prison classes.

> As you might guess, the majority of prison inmates fall into the Inadequate/Unworthy bottom-left quadrant with the **Victimentos.** Their sense of unworthiness stems directly from horrendous upbringings. Abuse at home is compounded by inferior education, pervasive racism, and, ultimately, lack of decent job opportunities. Given all of the above, it is often realistic for Victimentos to feel overwhelmed by life's challenges. Some Victimentos manage to rise above their conditioning, pull themselves up by their bootstraps, achieve authentic success, and transform themselves into Gung Hos—or, more accurately in such cases, Heroes.

> The Inadequate/Worthy bottom-right quadrant contains a mixture of **Impotentos.** They feel deserving of success, even entitled to it in many cases, but they don't know how to set about achieving it. A common ploy among Impotentos is to emulate the example of Obedio—you remember him—and catch on to the coattails of a strong leader. Impotentos typically feel deserving of success by virtue of the very same conformist qualities that simultaneously render them inadequate. They are also typically unrealistic.

Clearly, then, to possess an intact sense of self-esteem, one must feel both adequate and worthy. Since feelings of adequacy stem from truly knowing that one is capable of turning in a competent performance, building this element of self-esteem is merely a matter of acquiring know-how and honing skills. As noted, however, improved performance may not redeem a sense of unworthiness. That may require something akin to a metamorphosis. The key to that transformation lies in self-acceptance. Renée Richards, the tennis player, shared a lovely story concerning such a metamorphosis. "Being elected captain of the Yale tennis team seemed daunting. I worried that I wasn't really worthy of the honor, and that I might not be able to live up to it. But then one day, it hit me! 'Hey,' I thought, 'I actually *am* the captain of the Yale team. I might not be perfect, and I might not win every match but by definition, for this year anyway, I'm as good as it gets, and that's going to have to be quite good enough for anyone, including me.' And from that day forward, I never thought about it again."

A good way to keep that process going is to consider the way we present ourselves to others, along with our own feelings about ourselves. So, let's look at the responses that give some insight into yourself—or who you think you might be.

CALIBRATION	Q#	SENTENCE STEM
Mask	3	People think that I
Disposition	1	I am very
Talisman	26	The thing I like about myself is
Milestone	34	My most significant achievement
Rating	31	Compared with others, I

Your *Mask*—R3—is the image you present to the world. We seldom truly know what others think of us, so we mostly have to guess. And that guess is formed from how others respond to our presentation. We *project* the mask but never get to see it. We can only say for sure that we *assume* that other people see us as we *imagine* we project ourselves, and we usually underestimate other people's capacity to see through even the most carefully projected mask. Consider the following exchange. "What you need to understand about me is that I have a brilliant mind," said an acquaintance to a friend. "How dopey she must be," said the friend later, "to think that she's so much smarter than everyone else."

Wareham's Principle of the Opposite Image states that in order to know a person we should study the mask and ask ourselves, "What is the impression that this individual takes the greatest effort to convey to me?"—then work on the assumption that the true personality is the precise *opposite* of that. The bully is thus typically a coward, the clown a tragic figure, the loyal aide a duplicitous schemer. Within a prison setting, I have also seen firsthand that a polished mask of victimhood often signals a well-practiced capacity to present a fictitious sob story. The corollary is that the fellow who baldly admits his crimes is more likely to be authentic.*

The *Disposition*—R1—or self-image, is usually at odds with the Mask. If we were to string both of these sentences together, they might read, as one set did, "People think that I am a *bully* whereas in fact I am very *sensitive and caring*." The statement of disposition is much more reliable than the projected mask, for the responder is confiding, with any luck, how he truly feels about himself. Even though he might be lacking in insight, how he feels about himself will always be more reliable than how he imagines others feel about him.

The *Talisman*—R26—is something we generally carry in a pocket next to the heart. The talisman generally relates to an inner quality such as courage, ambition, aggression, or sensitivity. We often rely upon the talisman to guide and shape our fate in tight situations.

The *Ranking*—R31—is how we imagine we relate to others, mostly those in our immediate circle. The ranking, while not as unreliable as the mask, is nonetheless often decidedly wrong. Inmates commonly rank themselves too low. Mediocre corporate executives rank themselves far too high. And authentic achievers tend to correctly rank themselves as being reasonably average. The true ranking is thus often conveyed, to steal a word coined by United States President George W. Bush, *subliminably*.

Let's have a look at some actual cases, and you'll immediately appreciate how what we think about ourselves can imprison us.

---

*The Cubans catch this syndrome nicely with their saying, "Dime de lo que presumes y te diré lo que carecese."—Tell me what you brag about and I'll tell you what you lack.

PETER PRECIOUS

Peter	Q#	28, intelligent inmate in denial
Mask	3	People think that I am extremely gifted.
Disposition	1	I am very blessed.
Talisman	26	The thing I like about myself is the spirit of goodness resonating through my being.
Milestone	34	My most significant achievement is having the willingness to be the best I can be.
Ranking	31	Compared with others, I don't compare.

Peter, the only son of upper-middle-class parents, is a quick learner who almost graduated from a fine college. He projects himself as "extremely gifted," thereby immediately raising the question of whether he is as talented as he suggests or merely whistling in the dark. Like many such whistlers he fails to appreciate that others are just as smart, and all too often smarter. His pious statement of disposition—"I am very blessed"—disingenuously reinforces the mask of talented brilliance even as it pretends to humility. It is possible that "the spirit of goodness resonates" through Peter's being, but since he never truly admitted to responsibility for his crime—almost beating a man to death—his sincerity and self-insight are highly suspect. He is "willing" to be the best that he can be. Well, Big Deal. His ranking—"I don't compare myself to others"—is notably sanctimonious, for even in this limited selection of responses, Peter rates himself way, way ahead of others at every turn. In fact, Peter is felled by his own deceit. He wants to be seen as a brilliant sage precisely because he suffers a shaky sense of self-esteem. And, since a brilliant sage would not behave like a brute, he cannot admit to the brutish behavior for which he has correctly been incarcerated. At the end of his prison term, this highly intelligent and gentlemanly fellow has failed to grasp the central lesson of his own mistake. Even though he is about to be set free physically, so long as he remains in denial, he will remain incarcerated in a mental and emotional prison.

LARRY LEVIATHAN

Larry	Q#	45, high profile chief executive
Mask	3	People think that I can figure it out.
Disposition	1	I am very enthusiastic.
Talisman	26	The thing I like about myself is my sense of fair play.
Milestone	34	My most significant achievement was becoming a strong, humane chief executive, five days per week.
Ranking	31	Compared with others, I am more focused on the need to make a real contribution.

Larry didn't get to be a chief executive by accident. His projection of intellect and analysis is complemented by an enthusiastic disposition and a talisman of regard for fair play. These qualities of the head and heart are focused in a thoroughly adult way. Larry ranks himself according to his capacity to make a contribution, dedicates himself to being a humane chief executive, but remains cognizant of the need to maintain a happy family life. As you might guess, Larry went on to create a fine organization, a fortune for others, and a fine nest egg for himself and his family.

DWAYNE STRAIGHT

Dwayne	Q#	40, formerly violent felon
Mask	3	People think that I am doing okay, and I agree.
Disposition	1	I am very sensitive and focused.
Talisman	26	The thing I like about myself is my intelligence and sense of humor.

Milestone	34	My most significant achievement is being alive and turning my life around.
Rating	31	Compared with others, I used to come up short financially, but am now doing okay.

Dwayne has clearly emerged from an unhappy haze. Nowadays he is a productive, tax-paying citizen, and better equipped to deal with life's challenges than many high-flying executives. Dwayne projects himself truthfully, assesses himself realistically, believes in his own abilities, and is well on the way to fulfilling his dreams. The lessons of this profile can be summarized in four words: authenticity, insight, humility, and growth.

How to Escape the Prison of Negative Emotions

Each of us makes his own weather, determines the
color of the skies in the emotional universe he inhabits.
—Fulton J. Sheen

You'll recall that in the face of an obstacle, just about all executives respond that they simply surmount it. Prisoners, on the other hand, are inclined to give up, suffer feelings of anxiety, or succumb to temper tantrums. One way or another they advance to the rear. In fact, we all have to face difficult situations that evoke negative emotional reactions. It's the response to such dilemmas that differentiates the prisoner from the warrior. So let's peek at your mood-changers, as noted in the Wareham CLIQ.

CALIBRATION	Q#	MOOD-CHANGERS
Nirvana	30	I was happiest
Anxious	14	I become anxious
Guilty	20	I feel guilty
Depressed	32	I fall into a blue mood when

Irritated	25	I get irritated when
Angry	37	I lose my temper

If we're living life in the moment and have it under control, then these really are the good old days. Better than two out of three executives respond that they are happiest right now and three in ten specify being happiest at work. A similar number say they are happiest when with family or friends. For one in five, nirvana was school or college. For the balance, it was either the day of getting married or the day a child was born.

No prisoner responded that nirvana was in the here and now—which says something about prison life. Four out of ten said they were happiest either at work or when their lives were under control. One in four was happiest during childhood. One in three was happiest on the day of marriage or at the birth of a child.

The moral is that people who live in the past are not fully alive in the present. The golden era should ideally be right now. If not, then we should be thinking about making some changes.

Anxiety, for four in ten executives, is provoked by ambiguous business situations—new or unsolved problems, a plan going off the rails, and so on. An additional one in five reports feeling anxious in the face of a deadline. A further one in five gets anxious when personal performance falters. In essence, then, anxiety is provoked by the need to address the challenge at hand. And, as we've seen elsewhere, 90 percent of executives say that they go on to solve the problem.

Seven in ten prisoners become anxious in the face of everyday *survival* needs. And, intriguingly, one in five reports becoming anxious in the moment of being about to *win* something. For such people, *success itself becomes a tripwire*. Learning to deal with winning is a key issue for prisoners. They feel unworthy of success even when they know they have earned it. And, of course, if they win, their excuses, so central to their personality, cease to be valid. Little wonder, then, that so many would rather maintain the status quo.

Similar patterns hold true for guilt and depression. Essentially, however, these emotions are provoked by our own perceived inability to deal with life's challenges. We essentially direct our anger inward and blame ourselves.

Irritation and anger are different. Here the hostility is directed almost solely to others. Nearly half of all executives get irked by communications problems. An additional one in four complains of indecisiveness by others. The final one in four gets peeved by others' low standards. When it comes to anger, 70 percent of executives lose their cool when others fail, 10 percent are angered by personal failure, 10 percent claim to use anger as a conscious part of the grappling style, and the balance claim never to suffer a temper outburst. Among prisoners, one in ten gets angry with his own failures, and nine in ten lose their temper when lied to, disrespected, or endangered. One lesson is that prisoners are thin-skinned in the matter of disrespect. The other point worth making is that the ability to manage emotions is a key quality of great executives. The person who cannot manage emotion becomes imprisoned in the lowest echelons of corporate life, just as other thin-skinned individuals become incarcerated behind iron bars.

UNAPPRECIATED ARTISTS AND OVERWROUGHT EXECUTIVES

Even the shakiest among us can escape the prison of emotion. Consider twenty-year-old Troy in his green uniform, for example. "It's totally unfair," he wails. "I got arrested and thrown into jail for six months just because I did some graffiti. They didn't realize that I'm a serious artist."

Troy's underlying belief is that nothing bad would happen to him. Indeed, since the world should be fair, he might even be recognized by the public as a great artist and become a celebrity. This is a fine example of an irrational, imprisoning belief system. For in reality, the world is not always fair, and even if it were, applying graffiti to private or public property would still be a criminal act of vandalism from which certain consequences would inexorably flow.

If Troy could replace his irrational, imprisoning beliefs with realistic *liberating* beliefs, then several things would happen. First, he would accept responsibility for his actions. Second, reason would calm him and he would cease to wail. Third, he wouldn't put himself in the same position in the future.

This same basic concept—that the application of reason can spare us needless trouble, ease emotional distress, and make us better human beings—applies every bit as well within the corporate world. Consider Richard Ratchet.

RICHARD RATCHET

Richard	Q#	50, corporate executive
Nirvana	30	I was happiest when I was winning.
Anxious	14	I become anxious when I screw up.
Guilty	20	I feel guilty when haven't given 100 percent.
Depressed	32	I fall into a blue mood when I let myself down by saying something stupid.
Irritated	25	I get irritated when they say one thing and do another.
Angry	37	I lose my temper if I need to.

Richard's mood-changers reflect a whole cluster of imprisoning beliefs.

➤ Since he can only enter his *Nirvana*—R30—by winning, Richard has set himself up for precisely the kinds of imprisonment reflected in his other responses. If he could realize that *nobody* can win all the time, and that in any event we usually learn more from losing than winning, then he could begin to accept himself and frame his perspective in terms of contributing rather than merely competing.

➤ He says he gets anxious when he "screws up." The underlying imprisoning belief is that he should never screw up. But that's foolish. Why should Richard have to be any different than anyone else? An executive must take risks. And the more risks he takes, the more frequently he's going to fail. If he could absorb that insight—that liberating belief—Richard's anxiety would be eased.

➤ He feels guilty when he doesn't give 100 percent. Hey, the idea that we have to give 100 percent every single day is both irrational and imprisoning.

- He gets depressed when he says something stupid. But, hey, he just did. It is silly to believe that a person can get through a week (or even a day) without saying something stupid.

- He gets irritated when people say one thing but do another. Hang on there, Richard, in the real world that's what people do. So scrap the idea that people always ought to tell the truth—whatever that might be. Become a better judge of human nature and incorporate the notion that a little hypocrisy is an intrinsic part of human nature, and you'll become a better executive.

- He loses his temper when he needs to. The irrational, imprisoning belief—which locks him into an angry cage—is that Richard needs to lose his temper, presumably to get his way. In fact, we don't need to lose our temper at all. We can kill in cold blood if we want. And though things done in a fit of temper sometimes result in a quick fix, they all too often unravel further down the line—or even come back to haunt one's health.

Well, you get the picture. So examine your own mood-changers, identify the irrational beliefs that are imprisoning you, and feel free to embark on a whole new journey. But for now I'll let Nurturio tell you about that.

Nurturio's 7-Point Salvo

1. Begin this journey by accepting yourself, as you are right now, utterly without reservation. Don't be confused by appearances. Realize that you're a spiritual being having a physical experience, not merely a body having an emotional experience. Always remember that the power that governs the moon and stars, the trees and the flowers, the rise and fall of the tides and the movement of the seasons also flows through you. Now go to the mirror and take a long look at the mortal being who presently holds the key to your ultimate happiness. This is the person who for now has the capacity to choose what you will feel and think and do.

2. Never forget that you are infinitely more than your thoughts and feelings. These are just things that you experience. You will feel joy and you will feel pain. But bear in mind that suffering springs from perspective, so you are not the hapless victim of your earthly experiences and moods. You can change your disposition and your life in a moment. All you need to do is adjust your outlook. So learn to be gentle with yourself. Accept yourself on every level. See your faults as part of the perfection of being mortal. When forgiving others, include yourself.

3. Think well of yourself. Recognize your own value. Never put yourself down or call yourself names. Instead rejoice in the lessons you learn from your mistakes. Celebrate your talents, gifts, positive qualities, and successes. Think back on the many correct decisions you have made. Think at least one positive thought about yourself each night before sleeping. Then do the same again upon wakening. Add yourself to the list of your favorite people.

4. Depend on yourself. Accept responsibility for everything that happens in your life. Rely mostly upon yourself and give top priority to your own approval. Consider your own needs most important. Stand up for your rights. Learn to say no. Never forget that feelings of inadequacy are imposters that spring from the inside. They simply do not represent outside reality. Don't listen to skeptics. Dwell in your own palace or the world will be your jail. Heed the words of Buddha: "Let the wise man make of himself an island that no flood may overcome."

5. Never let your past define your present. Separate past suffering from present situations. Don't be a slave to your upbringing. Don't let the unhappy thoughts and feelings that directed you as a child propel your adult life. Learn from painful experiences but don't feel compelled to relive them. We only relive an experience because we have failed to fully learn its lessons. Don't compulsively identify yourself with your actions. You are not a mistake merely because you made one. Forgive yourself for all your gaffes, blunders, and missteps. Bury your grievances without a marker.

6. Revise your ideas about what you deserve. Consider your own opinion of yourself the most important. Define success in terms of what you want and never settle for second best. Resolve not just to survive but to express yourself and create love in your life. Never deny your own happiness. Bear in mind, however, that if you can be happy with nothing you possess everything, that if you can be free when down-trodden you can be free anywhere. So define yourself by your character rather than your accomplishments. And be patient with yourself. Change takes time.

7. Above all be authentic. Be the person you are, not the person others want you to be. Don't compare yourself with others. Never let being different or seeming different bother you. Don't stumble for fear of the impression you might convey. Don't change yourself merely to win approval. Think before you speak, avoid irksome half-truths and white lies, and share your honest opinion with empathy and tact.

Nurturio's Paradox

To be honest, I used to worry that Nurturio's homilies seemed a little naive. My skepticism has to do with my background. I've dedicated much of my life to spotting the hidden flaw within the executive psyche. I've seen too many shysters—in both prison greens and pinstripe suits—to blindly accept the notion that people are intrinsically perfect and don't need to change.

Time and again, I've been in the position of counseling clients to think long and hard—very long and very hard—before committing to some so-called executive who is masking feelings of inferiority behind an apparently serene "I love and accept myself" façade. I've seriously doubted that "pious admonitions" could really cure such wannabes. And if mere sermons could cure criminality, there'd be nobody in jail, right?

So, how, I demanded to know of Nurturio, does your doctrine of self-acceptance—and all the other touchy-feely stuff that springs from it—really alleviate a self-esteem problem? Nurturio didn't seem miffed at all by my imperious query. Instead he listened closely and heard me out in silence. Then, after some moments of deep thought, he offered the following answer in his soft and soothing voice:

> *A paradox comes into play. Every crisis can lead to transformation, though not every crisis does. Ultimately, however, self-acceptance becomes a choice imposed upon us by a final overwhelming predicament. And, in that very moment, making the fateful choice to accept ourselves just as we are, we embark upon the process of regeneration.*

CHAPTER 15

How to Preserve the Appearance of Integrity

When Push Comes to Shove

> The louder he talked of his integrity
> > the faster we counted our spoons.
>
> —Ralph Waldo Emerson

> It's not your word, it's who you give it to.
>
> —the cowboy character in Sam Peckinpah's film *The Wild Bunch*

Here's a real-world moral problem to ponder: A longtime employee and codirector who ran one of my offices took out a ten-year lease on our premises, and, without consulting me, gave his personal guarantee to secure what looked like favorable terms, a common-enough ploy in a hot property market. A few years later we relocated and with the landlord's assent assigned the lease to someone else. Alas, the business climate turned rotten, the sublessee fell into bankruptcy, the space couldn't be sublet again, and contrary to his earlier assurances, the landlord used the personal guarantee clause to lever damages from my colleague. The matter went to court and my codirector—a man now retired—was suddenly liable for nearly $100,000 in back rent and legal fees, a decent chunk of change today and a whole lot of money back then. Well, even though the lease had been executed in the name of my limited liability company, I hadn't been so silly as to give that personal guarantee, so I was off the hook. No one could extract that money from me. They'd have to squeeze it from my former employee's home and pension instead.

But was I really off the hook? Or was my probity dangling on that line? Let's think about integrity for moment.

Fools and Wise Men

Many people equate integrity with honesty, sincerity, or candor. In fact, to possess integrity a person has to be more than an honest fool.* Others say integrity is a matter of strict adherence to a deeply felt code of principles. By this definition cultists who follow their leaders to suicide are people of integrity. Well, it ain't necessarily so.

Nurturio is quick to point out, however, that real integrity is something deeper again and possesses a psychological element. Webster's mentions a condition of being, "untouched, unimpaired, entire." I like that word, *entire*.

According to Nurturio a person of integrity is an entire person, that is to say a mature adult. He understands the ways of the world. He realizes that virtually nothing is absolute. He understands temptation and he can feel it, too. He also knows, however, somewhere deep in his heart, that some decisions and some outcomes are just plain wrong.

He's a member of humanity connected to the rest of us. Because he can see the real world he understands human vulnerabilities. In assessing a course of action, he takes the long view; he wants things to turn out right for the other fellow—precisely because he senses that when that happens they'll likely turn out right for him, too.

He'll not take advantage of any other's weaknesses because he knows that this would deprecate the value of all human relationships, and therefore redound to his ultimate disadvantage. The tacit understanding that informs his dealings is that each of us is looking out not just for No.1, but for the other person also.

Words and Weasels

In everyday business dealings integrity usually hinges on the matter of honoring one's word. When we say someone is a person of his word, we mean more than that he simply keeps his word. We mean, too, that he understands what he's said, and that he intends to stick to both the word and spirit of the agreement struck, even though doing so might render him, one way or another, out of pocket. We know that he would

---

*Eternal skeptic Ambrose Bierce defined truthful as "dumb and illiterate," which is pretty funny when you think about it.

rather lose his money than his integrity—which he believes would be the certain consequence of failing to keep his word.

In the "real world" such sentiments can seem like luxuries, so a lot of people pretend to be exponents of the "win-win" deal while secretly plotting the downfall of their "opponents"—by means, for example, of any of the following stratagems:

> **Getting into an essentially irreversible relationship precisely in order to be able to come back and "renegotiate" key items later.** Many marriages have been founded on this basis, hence the increasing popularity of the prenuptial agreement.

> **Inserting a penalty clause that is really no penalty at all.** Then, simply breaking the agreement and paying the penalty. I first heard of this ruse from a brilliant—if ultimately ill-fated—lawyer, whose sophistry seldom failed to surprise.

> **Sweetening the pot.** Who would dare whisper the word *bribe* in connection with Newt Gingrich's five-million-dollar book contract with Rupert Murdoch (or even Gingrich's $300,000 loan from Bob Dole)? Murdoch is the master of such sweetenings, of course, as witness his hiring of the Mayor of New York's ex-wife as a news anchor right at the moment of needing Mr. Guiliani's support to crush Ted Turner's stranglehold on Manhattan's cable news. (To be fair to Guiliani, he kept up his end of this bargain, thereby perhaps exemplifying the old adage that an honest politician is someone who stays true to the first person who paid him.)

> **Appointing a shill.** Harvey Mackay, in his best-selling *Swim With the Sharks*, counsels—with a straight face, too—that the best way to win a great property deal is to have some kind of shill tender a series of bad-faith offers to plumb the vendor's rock-bottom selling price; then of course, the shill disappears into the woodwork, and you, smiling innocently, enter through the front door armed with all the necessary knowledge to secure the bargain price—or maybe even chisel a little more off it.

> **Introducing a note of calculated ambiguity.** Uriah Heep cheated his boss by "cooking the books." Outside of Hollywood this is illegal and

mostly a no-no. A not unknown variant, however, is to secure control of the purse strings and then fail to keep or ever produce any books. This way, nobody actually "knows" what is happening, and the Uriah-in-process can pretend—even to himself—to be doing the right thing by everyone.

> **Deserving a special deal.** Alan Bond, the Aussie real-estate-magnate-cum-criminal* who used Sotheby's own money to purchase Van Gogh's *Iris* at auction, came up with a truly creative way of rationalizing his subsequently revealed white-collar criminal behavior. He pleaded diminished responsibility, explaining that a "nervous break-down" had caused his IQ to plummet from a mind-boggling 180 to an idiot 70. Bond didn't escape jail, but the Aussie judge—perhaps succumbing to more than mere blandishment—handed down the lightest of sentences. The perspicacity in this ruse, of course, lay less in the self-effacing admission of a jellifying brain than the audacious claim to an initial genius-level IQ.

Signals and Omens

The world is full of wonderful people and I'm delighted to confide that I've met my full share of them. One way or another, I've also met more weasels than I'd ever quite anticipated, but none of those slippery critters, so far anyway, has opened with an avowal of his dissembling skills (though, to be fair, I've heard a few straight-faced paraphrasings of Groucho Marx's line, "Those are my principles, and if you don't like them I have others."). In the absence of such an engaging admission, you might look askance upon:

> **Avowals of integrity, honesty, et al.** One in five executive candidates typically opens the discussion with a declaration of his integrity. Not a smart strategy: the matter of the fellow's integrity was never at issue until he raised the question. And, of course, he likely raised it precisely because the matter rested uneasily within his conscience. Look with a jaundiced eye, too, on any unsolicited heartfelt affirmation that you, in the course of any

---

*For the record Mr. Bond was born in the United Kingdom and emigrated to Australia as a child (and effectively never grew out of that happy state).

dealing with a person of such so-called integrity will never be "cheated or harmed."

- ➤ **Any mention of a gentleman's agreement.** I wince whenever I hear this expression; a gentleman, after all, never uses the word. And, of course, just about anyone who refers to a gentleman's agreement realizes that a gentleman's word is worth more than his own and usually wants to hold you to the higher standard.

- ➤ **Reluctance to put an agreement in writing.** Paradoxically, a wise man, realizing the implications of a verbal agreement, is often quicker than most to reduce his word to writing, thereby to avoid any misunderstandings. More often than not it's the shifty operator who says, Trust me, my word is my bond. He wants you to take him at his word precisely because he knows he'll feel free to weasel out of it later.

- ➤ **Any deal that looks too good to be true.** The natural enemy of integrity is temptation. A deal that looks too good to be true usually springs from the inherent greedy wish to profit from someone else's misfortune. Block that feeling, for, as the saying goes, an honest man can't be conned.

Prophylactics and Consequences

Very few reflective executives seriously claim the halo of absolute integrity; they know it is mostly an ideal to be pursued. That's not always good enough for Nurturio, however. He's always stressing the importance of authenticity and "walking the talk." He and Cogitato got together one day and concocted a set of rules for staying out of trouble, thereby permitting the other member of that splendid trinity, Advancio, to consistently preserve at least the appearance of integrity. Alas, these dictums haven't always worked. Advancio hasn't always observed all of them, either. But Nurturio never quite lets the matter drop, and in the long term everyone's been very grateful to him for that. So, here then are those very simple rules:

- ➤ First, realizing the wisdom of the adage that nobody can let you down unless you're leaning on them, try not to strike hard bargains. The best deal is something everybody wants and can live with.

> Second, be impeccable with your word, and don't make careless or offhand promises. Why risk the prospect of a thoughtless pledge coming home to haunt you?

> Third, get everything down on paper. As my father liked to say, "Now, if you'll just sign here on the dotted line, why then we really will have a gentleman's agreement."

Finally, of course, once you've given your word, stick to it—taking care to remind yourself of the spirit of the understanding reached. That was how I came to shell out the $100,000 for which my codirector was technically liable.* We'd never discussed the matter, but he knew he had my permission to act on my behalf in any way he felt best. He also knew me well enough to know that I'd likely have given my personal guarantee (albeit reluctantly) to secure that particular piece of office space at that particular time. I just wasn't around and he had to move quickly so he selflessly put his name and signature on the line. I also so greatly respected my colleague's personal integrity—as you would've, too, if you'd known him—that I could never've held up my head in his presence had I reneged on our tacit contract to look out for each other.

---

*I needed that money, by the way, so coughing up was a hardship.

CHAPTER 16

How to Create Some Love in Your Life
& Discover It in Unexpected Places

Love is the child of freedom, never that of domination

—Eric Fromm

Nurturio's voice can be very comforting when things go wrong. Like the night I got arrested—which, whenever I recall it, I relive.

My wife and I are journeying home from a Broadway show. The subway turnstile gags on my newly purchased Metro card (a digital fare card). The crowd is pressing, and my wife, her own card in hand, peers over my shoulder. Suddenly, the turnstile bar abruptly swings, hurtling us, as one person, on to the subway platform. Not grasping what has happened, my wife surges ahead with the crowd to the escalator.

An angry voice breaks the air, "Hey you!" I hesitate and glance back over my shoulder. "Call that woman back," commands the voice.

I have paid to enter the subway, so I have committed no crime. And since Margaret is oblivious to the fact that we've both gone through on one fare, neither has she. But there is a problem. We've recently applied for American citizenship so I don't want this incident to mistakenly mar that application.

"Which woman?" I ask.

Three muftied minions suddenly appear before me. A bellicose officer in casual clothes struts into my space. He'd been standing outside on the street, separated from the subway by iron bars. He brandishes a badge. "You're under arrest," he snarls.

"What's the charge?"

"Theft of services."

I hold up my Metrocard. "I paid my fare."

"You were with that woman. *She* didn't pay." No laws have been broken, but somehow this jut-jawed, in-your-face official fails to inspire confidence. I decide to remain silent. "You're under arrest, you hear! So where's your ID?"

Alas, I'm carrying only my Metrocard, a theater program, and a five-dollar bill.

He snaps the handcuffs on me, brandishes his walkie-talkie, and calls for a paddy wagon. Now I'm cuffed, frisked, and traipsed into the Broadway lights where I attract odd, embarrassed looks from the subway hordes, and ponder the irony of my predicament. Why would the fates incarcerate the creator of a class for prison inmates? That's when I hear Nurturio's voice.

Relax, you're embarking upon an intriguing journey. It'll be good for you to see exactly what your students have to go through.

They take me to the Midtown booking station, relieve me of my shoelaces, belt and tie, then photograph and fingerprint me before finally tossing me into a dark holding cell, containing a silver-haired, sagelike African-American. Could it be he?

"How's *your* evening been, then, Nurturio?" I ask.

"Well, Ah'm Orpheus, actually, and Ah'm homeless," he responds. "Ah hope to be out in time to hustle breakfast."

I phone my wife. Assuming I was somewhere on the train too, she'd boarded the waiting downtown N train—and alighted to a terrifying scene from the film *The Vanishing*.

Shortly after midnight, Orpheus and I and two other venerable citizens, cuffed behind our backs, are crammed into the back row of a customized minibus. Seven police officers fill the front three rows. The driver, a frustrated Grand Prix star apparently, careens the vehicle across Manhattan toward the West Side Highway at fifty-plus miles per hour. Other than to hit the accelerator and sound a burst on the siren at the red lights on the avenues, this daredevil is oblivious to others on the road. It's a chase scene from a bad movie. The twisting asphalt rushes to the windshield. Orpheus's fragile frame jams into the left side of my ribcage and my right ear presses into the side window as we swing onto the West Side Highway. Our pilot revs the volume on a tape of boom-boom salsa and jams his foot to the floor. My gleeful captors cheer him on as we vanquish all comers in the race downtown.

People don't always behave the way they should, says Nurturio, so just forgive them and enjoy the ride.

At around 1:00 A.M. we clamber down a dingy iron stairwell into the "Tombs," the infamous underground maze that imprisons persons convicted of no offense while they await a first hearing. The guards are a mixture. Some are keen enough to help, but many are as surly as reluctant circus animals. Several are unnecessarily churlish and autocratic.

It's a demanding job, so don't be quick to judge them by their attitudes, says Nurturio.

My cuffs are removed and I get back my tie, belt, and shoelaces. The Tombs come as a surprise: invasive fluorescent lights, freshly painted hospital-green walls and bars, freshly disinfected, sparkling gray concrete floors. I share 200 square feet of cell with eighteen inmates. Half a dozen have commandeered the two-foot-wide stainless steel bench that snakes the cell perimeter. The rest seek repose on the floor. A gleaming stainless steel toilet bowl occupies a corner. A pay phone juts from the wall. Orpheus presses a quarter into my hand. I tell my wife I'll be okay.

My mind races. Who'd ever dare take issue with our Mayor's potent crime-crushing policies? He's a classic rule-by-fear, quick-results leader. He'd perhaps not approve of the hair-raising race to the Tombs—yet in a way he already did, for his minions know what they can get away with, and know he'll look the other way if anyone complains. But no matter, for where's the harm in the inadvertent incarceration of an apparent turnstile beater—or anyone without proper ID, for that matter—so long as the city's made safe for decent people? I insinuate myself under the steel bench, fashion my jacket into a pillow, and seek answers.

At 4:00 A.M. there's breakfast: corn flakes, milk, and an apple. I survey the diners. Half are in for quality-of-life crimes: carrying an open beer can, smoking weed, urinating behind a truck in a public parking lot, driving-license anomalies, turnstile jumping. . . . Orpheus's crime is vagrancy. Four are would-be armed robbers. One proudly displays an old war wound, a wicked shot in the back. "I'll be on the Island," he says. "How do I qualify for your class?" Orpheus gets an early court call. I produce my five-dollar bill. "Here's breakfast, Nurturio."

"I'll go by any name you say, man, but from this point on you're on your own." He smiles. "There'll be nothing you can't deal with, I'm sure."

At three o'clock I'm called upstairs into a grungy steel-doored confessional. "Accept an immediate conditional dismissal," says an assigned legal-aid defender. "All record of your arrest will be expunged. You could sue the city, but you'd be looking at investing time and money."

A dozen inmates on my side of the grate pace the floor. Carl, now forty-one, has been in and out of prison since age eighteen. His front teeth are missing, he's overweight, and has no marketable skills. Yet he's a nice guy, intelligent, too. He declines the offer of community service. "I'd be working without pay. I'd never support myself. I'm better off at Rikers." A thirty-one-year-old construction worker says that when his wife got pregnant he couldn't afford to pay a parking fine so his license got suspended. No problem, so long as she drove the car. But when the time came to drive her to the hospital, he took the wheel. He got pulled over on a DWB, Driving While Black. Now he's lost a day's work—$120. I tell him my story and his face lights up. "Hey! Now *you* know how the police treat *us!*"

"Every day of our lives," chimes a winsome West Indian. "You've gotta tell them."

"Yes, people don't believe us, but they'll believe you." All this innocent faith in my powers is touching and depressing.

I accept the judge's dismissal—and head for the door with my wife.
So what did you learn, then, asks Nurturio?
That innocent people can be incarcerated.
That's not enough.

My wife and I stroll out into a sunny late-spring afternoon. Trees are verdant and birds are singing. I'm relieved, exultant even. Freedom—never take it for granted. I stop stock-still. "We're walking atop the Tombs," I explain. "The prisoners are beneath our feet, literally." Indeed. A hapless mass of quality-of-life offenders, the wretched refuse of our gleaming city, our truly needy, our tired and poor, incarcerated but not yet convicted, neatly packed together within sturdy iron bars set into shimmering, freshly disinfected concrete floors, are huddled, hurting, and yearning to breathe free, right now.
What else did you learn?
I learned that in modern Manhattan the cop preempts justice, and proportionality is a lost value. In Mr. Giuliani's New York, as in Mr. Lee Kuan Yew's Singapore, virtually any perceived offense may carry

automatic arrest and incarceration. That's quite a penalty. What judge would jail anyone for $1.50? But the Red Queen's rules apply: punishment first, injustice later. I see with my own eyes that innocent people really do get hurt in such a system. Cops really do exceed their mandates. The cost of a private lawyer to fight a wrongful arrest will be at least a thousand dollars and a day off work. For some, like me, it doesn't much matter. I can stomach a glitch in the system. I can overlook an illegal race to the Tombs. I can afford an attorney. I can wrest value from a day without work. But others less fortunate are sorely punished. The arrest record is capriciously swollen and our Big Brother world can be unforgiving—legally, financially, and emotionally. The wronged person feels impotent and joins an embittered, alienated underclass. I learned all that.

You didn't learn enough.

I learned that the problem was systemic. That individual officers, motivated to maintain arrest quotas, have lost all sense of proportionality. They act as judge and jury dispensing severe on-the-spot punishments. What judge, really, would ever sentence anyone to jail time for turnstile jumping? Or even mete out a fine to match a day or two of lost work?

Anything else?

I think I'm beginning to realize that the Demandio style of Manhattan's jut-jawed Mayor Rudolph Giuliani offers a quick fix for the crime rate, but that less quantifiable issues will come back to haunt us.

I learned to seize the best in whatever comes my way.

There are more important lessons for you to learn.

When will I learn them?

You said it yourself—when the student is ready the teacher appears.

Two days later I was back on Rikers Island for my regular weekly class. There's a highly effective grapevine out there so everyone knew of my arrest. The incident had made me something of a hero, actually. I open the class with a droll joke. "Fellow inmates," I say to laughter and applause. I then explain that getting handcuffed and spending the night in "the Tombs" has taught me some useful lessons. In recalling the experience, however, I suddenly begin to relive it.

This time though, things are different. This time I feel deep, deep anger at having been clapped in handcuffs, traipsed out under the bright Broadway lights to wait for the paddy wagon to take me away to share a cell with the so-called dregs of society. This time, not being able to use my hands makes me feel helpless, vulnerable, and desperately undignified, ashamed—even, I imagine, something like being displayed in the public stocks. This time the stares of passing theatergoers make me want to cry out that I was merely the innocent victim of a terrible mistake.

See, we only truly know what we experience. Thinking's not enough. We have to feel our way to growth. That's the whole point of suffering. It teaches things that we can never otherwise learn.

"You okay there, teach?"

Thirty pairs of empathetic eyes watch me emerge from my catatonic nightmare. I choke back a lump in my throat and the welling of tears in my eyes. The class realizes—they *know*—that I'm more shaken up by my incarceration than I quite realize. Empathizing with my unresolved feelings and incipient tears, they permit me to gather myself and move directly to the day's lesson, Adler's seminal paper on feelings of inferiority.

Okay then, Nurturio. Jailing in and of itself merely evoked feelings of hurt, shame, resentment, and anger. And understanding isn't enough. Compassion, for me, anyway, comes from sharing not just a cell but also a long-term classroom with a so-called bunch of criminals. I've learned that most of these lost souls are intelligent, caring, decent human beings whose antisocial tendencies mostly spring from battering upbringings.

Max DePreez, chairman and chief of Herman Miller Inc., noted in his book, *Leadership Is an Art*, "Managers who understand only methodology and quantification are modern-day eunuchs who can never engender competence or confidence. Were we to keep 'becoming' as individuals," he says, "we would be better off as persons and as institutions." The same can be said of criminals. They're skilled outlaws but impotent citizens. Their salvation—like everyone else's—lies in growth, not mere incarceration.

I've seen firsthand the power of mere presence as a nurturing tool.

One day I had each of my inmate students give a three-minute speech entitled "The story of my life." With good humor and no complaints, speaker after speaker related the stories of dysfunctional childhoods and descents into hell—yet showed remarkably little insight into how the grim upbringing had ultimately come back to effect his incarceration.

One fellow, Santos, in prison for beating up his wife and her lover, told of seeing, as an eight-year-old, the only person who had ever shown him any love, his grandmother, being fatally set aflame by his own step-siblings.

Every speaker ran beyond the allotted three-minute limit, but I didn't have the heart to cut anybody off. Finishing the story seemed vital to the exercise.

Finally, with just one minute left in the session I struggled to my feet. "I've borne witness to your lives," I said. "We all have. You probably don't realize how important it was to get your history out into the open. The good news is that you're victims of your upbringing, just like everyone else. The bad news is that now that you've told your story it can no longer excuse your behavior. There's no choice except to get over it and create a new life. See you next week."

On the way out the door Santos grabbed my hand. "I'm learning so much," he said, beaming. "Your class is the greatest."

In fact, since everyone's presentations had run over-time, I'd given up on the scheduled lesson. All I'd done was listen.

How to Greet Strangers

Love is but the discovery of ourselves in others,
and the delight in the recognition.
—Alexander Smith

"However do you get them to do that?" Howard, the chief of a major corporation, has just attended a formal parliamentary debate at Rikers among the inmates—and he's perplexed.

"How do I teach them to become great debaters?"

"No, I can figure that out for myself. What I want to know is how do you get them to be so friendly? I mean they just walked up to me, introduced themselves, shook hands, and treated me like a friend. They *all* did! You taught them to do that, right?"

I was struck by the question. I'd never attempted to instruct any class member in the art of greeting strangers. I reflected that, like many leaders, Howard had probably shied away from getting too close to his followers—and they him—and that was perhaps why an outpouring of uninhibited friendship came as a surprise. Mulling his question later, however, I remembered that the class wasn't always so friendly. In the beginning, many were shy, reluctant to speak, and standoffish. In an unconscious effort to deal with this, I reflexively made a point of shaking the hand of every class member. Soon enough, the handshakes—along with high-fives and in some cases belly-bumps—were coming from the class members themselves. And that's how, without my saying a single word, my class, or most of them, anyway, learned to befriend anyone, even captains of industry.

The Paradox of Love and Friendship

Since I've seen more affection in a prison classroom than in many middle-class homes, it wouldn't surprise me to discover that a key element of recidivism is the wish to return to a friendly and loving place. As Santos remarked to me following one class, "It's lonelier in the city than on the Island."

Creating love in one's life does not come easy to sufferers of low self-esteem. But if we can do it, self-esteem rises.

Love has many dimensions, including romance, camaraderie, everyday goodwill, and, of course, love of family.

One quick way to get a handle on the condition of your love relationships is to enter your responses to the Wareham CLIQ below:

CALIBRATION	Q#	LOVE RELATIONSHIPS
Father	5	My father
Paternal Vacuum	6	If only my father
Mother	8	My mother
Maternal Vacuum	9	If only my mother
Longing	18	What I need most in a partner is

First, look for *negative* responses. *Any* criticism of either parent probably reflects unresolved inner conflict that you need to contemplate and address.

Now, look for a correlation between the *Parental Vacuums*—R6 and R9—and the quality you long for—the *Longing*—R18—in a partner or friend.

Most people unconsciously hope to find a partner who will provide the very thing that their parents did not. Bear in mind that both partners in a relationship possess such unconscious longings. Neither partner, however, has the *right* to expect the other to tend to those longings, not on a long-term basis, anyway.

Sure, partnership is about caring for each other. But to feel entitled to lean on another person consistently is a sure-fire formula for trouble.

The same kinds of rules apply to our everyday friendships, because we often mistakenly expect our friends to satisfy our unconscious longings and needs. In describing our friends we typically describe ourselves, too.

It is a paradox, but the way to get what we need to ease our longings involves accepting and giving—first through a conscious effort to accept others exactly as they are, warts and all, and second, by contributing to the world at large.

Nurturio should be heeded closely in this area of relationships. The last time I spoke to him he offered up what he called his four pillars of friendship.

NURTURIO'S FOUR PILLARS

The way to have a friend is to be one. There is no greater impediment to friendship than not being at ease with yourself. So instead of *searching* for the right person dedicate your energy to *becoming* the right person. Observe in yourself the compulsion to go back to the same unhappy people for the same unhappy rejections—then rid yourself of it, for no one can walk over you unless you are lying down. When you become the right person the right friend will appear, and you both will know it. Looks can be deceiving, so make a real effort to see friends instead of enemies in the faces of strangers. Remember that life is a mirror that reflects our own countenance, so make a happy face and see a happy world. Don't take a long face or old wounds to a new relationship. Never take the miracle of friendship for granted. If you miss a friend and haven't heard from him, then make the effort to reach out.

Treat everyone as your equal. No one is above you and no one is below you. To think that way is to alight upon a lonely shelf. If you are already lonely, this may be the reason why. So, just as you should hold no head higher than your own, so, too, you should embrace diversity and accept people as they are, not as you want them to be. Never forget that the way to rid yourself of a friend is to try to improve him. Satisfy the urge to change others by changing yourself. Change your attitude, not your friend. Look for the best in people. Think and speak kindly of others.

Expect conflict. See imperfection as humanity itself. See faults as wounds, with compassion not anger. Remain calm in the face of hysteria by reminding yourself that an angry person is merely trying to survive. Never forget that other people always have logical reasons for what they say and do. The logic may be unclear to you—it may even be totally wrong—but, for the moment, anyway, it is very clear to the other person. So remain calm, say nothing, and listen.

Let go of the burden of always being right. Choose to be happy rather than to be right. Notice your own faults in others. Don't rationalize, *apologize*. Make a conscious effort to see the other perspective, and then seriously contemplate the current problem in that light. Accept compliments graciously and pay careful attention to criticism. Reject unkind remarks cheerfully but not out of hand. Be prepared to be comfortably wrong. Welcome any justifiable blame that comes your way; it is surely a gift that will make you a better person. Now compliment your enemy, throw a party instead of a fit, accommodate his needs into your own, and help him to get what he wants. Miracles will follow.

CHAPTER 17

Games Recidivists Play

& How to Pick Up and Go Home

Repeating mistakes is more likely than profiting from them.

—Malcolm Forbes

Areal-life recidivist's underlying beliefs can seem depressingly banal. Corporate inmates have essentially the same beliefs, however. They just make their self-sabotaging utterances sound a tad more reasonable. Convicts complain about the world, the country, and the politicians. Corporate inmates direct their ire toward the market, the industry, the corporation, and the leadership team. And so it goes. In the hope of reaching both groups with one last shot then, let's consider a compendium of games recidivists play.

1. DISMAL WORLD

The core imprisoning belief in Dismal World is that "The outlook is dismal and the world is rotten." Various qualifiers may be added: "America (or for corporate inmates, 'this industry') is the worst of the rotten, and causing most of the problems in the world. New York (or 'this corporation')—might just be the rottenest city in the universe." The corollary is that "the bad guys are in charge and everything is unfair." The refrain is well known: "Oh-my-God—ain't it *awful*!"

An "iffy alibi" inevitably underlies each game. In Dismal World the alibi is that "I'm a living testament to what I say; I've failed precisely because the bad guys are in charge and the world really is rotten."

The key to any game is the unconscious emotional prism through which the inmate perceives the world. In Dismal World the filter is the continuing pain from childhood wounds. The grappling style is whining passivity.

As we've seen, a crucial key to releasing oneself from prison is to replace imprisoning beliefs with realistic, liberating counter-beliefs. The counter-belief for players trapped in Dismal World is this: "The world may not be entirely beautiful or to my liking, but I can create a good life for myself and enjoy the many wonderful things that life has to offer."

2. HOODWINKED

Hoodwinked players believe "there's a huge conspiracy going on."

Corporate inmates usually restrict the conspiracy to senior management along with the directors and auditors. Actual inmates are not so restrained. In fact, the size of the plot is usually crucial to the game. Players whisper—and sometimes shout—that *all* our supposed leaders and politicians are in on the scheme and conspiring against the common man. The system itself is part of the conspiracy, they say, especially, the banks, news media, courts, judges, police, wardens, and correctional officers.

It is impossible for an onlooker to query the validity of the game, either by pointing to the millions of people who haven't been victimized by the conspiracy, or by pointing to the highly placed officials within the system whose integrity is well-known. In face of such rationality, Hoodwinked players merely introduce the substantiating corollary: "That's the point! It's precisely because the conspiracy is so cunning and so pervasive that so many people have either been duped, or are paid-off traitors."

Unfortunately, Hoodwinked players never apply that kind of unrelenting intellect to the value of their own underlying iffy alibi, "The conspiracy has rendered me powerless, *that's* why I can't get out of prison or ahead in the world." The underlying emotional prism to the Hoodwinked is exclusion. Hoodwinked players felt excluded from society growing up, and in consequence feelings of helplessness dominate. The grappling style might be characterized as "knee-jerk authority-kicker."

Liberating counter-beliefs—which typically merely evoke the disdainful cry: "They've got *you* fooled"—include the following:

➤ It is normal for people to meet and pursue common goals.

- Human nature being what it is, conflicts of interest and corruption are inevitable.

- We live in a flawed democracy—as democracies inevitably are—but the power to vote people out of office is nonetheless real, and the news media compete vigorously to reveal conflicts of interest and corruption.

- Nowadays the Internet can spread the truth to the world for nickels so everybody has a voice and conspiracies are becoming virtually impossible to contain.

- I can make a difference and be part of the group that changes things we don't like.

3. HARD PLACE

The core belief that puts Hard Place players between a rock and hard place is simply this: "I had no choice but to break the law." Arthur Andersen auditors are saying much the same thing following the Enron debacle.

Given sympathy they go on to explain, "I was caught in a bind and victimized for doing what I had to. I simply had to survive and there was no other way to make that happen." Ambitious players offer a variant: "I'm as entitled to top dollar as anyone else, and the only way for me to get that is to resort to cheating or violence or crime."

"Given my situation, the law should not apply," is the iffy alibi. Practiced players sometimes go on to say, "I should be pitied, not punished." More daring players extend that argument, saying, "The law is at fault and should be changed, so I am actually a revolutionary who deserves praise."

These excuses refract from an emotional prism of injured self-esteem, which has obliterated the capacity to contemplate success within the social structure. The obsolete grappling style is compulsive corruption or criminality.

The liberating counter-beliefs are these: "My inability to see other options lead to my unethical or criminal behavior, and that landed me in trouble," and "I can learn new things and create a whole range of decent options for myself in the future."

4. KICK ME

Kick Me players seldom sing, but their core imprisoning belief is the title of a popular song, "Everybody's Always Picking on Me."

Kick Me takes pride in revealing the individual identities of those within the heartless throng who did them wrong or are planning to. "My parents picked on me then kicked me out," they say. "Then my school-teachers picked on me and got the head honcho to expel me. My boss picked on me and fired me." Prison inmates go on to explain that "the police picked on me and the judge kicked me into prison where the correctional officers stuck me in the 'Why Me' pen. The parole officer will pick on me then kick me back inside. Employment officers ignore me, or if I ever get employed the boss will pick on me and kick me out."

The iffy alibi is that "since mean-spirited people keep on getting me into trouble I'm to blame for nothing." The answer to the query as to why everyone is so vindictive is the wide-eyed avowal that "*I* sure as hell don't know *that.*" The emotional prism is the need for attention; any is better than none, so it is better to find a way to be picked on than to do nothing and be ignored. The obsolete grappling style is "compulsive provocateur."

The liberating counter-beliefs are these: "*I'm* responsible for the way people treat me so I can act in such a way that they will treat me well. In any event, I don't need to take anything personally and nobody can insult me without my consent."

5. MISTER COOL

Mister Cool finds pride and comfort in his core imprisoning belief, "being a thug—or an executive who can command a limousine—is cool." That notion of detached panache creates a sense of identity and invests his life with meaning. He has effectively appropriated Descartes's dictum, "I think therefore I am," and turned it on its ear. Now it reads "I am a thug—or a corporate officer—therefore I am cool." The corollary immediately follows: "I am happy to live and die as a thug. Jail is part of thug life, too, but I am so cool and so tough that I accept that." Ultimately, players of Mister Cool—Coolies—convince themselves to believe that "All things considered, I'm having a pretty good life, so I don't need to change."

The iffy alibi is this: "I'm imprisoned precisely because I'm tough and cool." Again, the emotional prism is the abused and wounded self-esteem that precludes the ability to see another life. The obsolete grappling style for inmates is that of the bullying, macho sociopath; for corporate inmates it is obsessive concern with unfulfilling power and status.

The liberating counter-beliefs are these: "Being a thug—or staying in a job that fails to fulfill—will ultimately destroy my human value. Life would be more rewarding and less hassle if I were getting everything I want by using my deepest talents to make a contribution, living the kind of life I'd really like to live—and I can make that happen."

6. NO EXIT

To join in the game of No Exit, the player simply takes to heart the imprisoning belief we initially heard from Alberto, "There's no turning back now," and then go on to recite this mantra: "I cannot beat the system. I cannot get where I want to go. This miserable life is all I can hope for. I have burned all my bridges. My past is obvious to others. There are no opportunities for anyone with my record or resume." The iffy alibi is obvious: "To attempt to change is pointless so I've no choice but to go on doing exactly what I've always done."

This is a game favored by countless neurotics who claim they're damaged beyond redemption by past events and have absolutely no control over their unhappy circumstances, pendulum moods, angry outbursts, outrageous behaviors, and irrational, imprisoning beliefs. Spotting the hidden payoff is a snap: as long as they cling to such thought patterns, victim status is assured.

Again, the emotional prism is injured self-esteem. They're unwilling to accept responsibility for leading a productive life in the area of their authentic desires. So the same old self-defeating grappling style— which may take many forms—remains rigidly in place.

The liberating counter-belief is that the enlightened public at large welcomes the concept of self-redemption. They *want* to believe that offenders can be rehabilitated. If the No Exit ex-offender could accept this, he could also realize that people will accept him as they find him. Then, with luck, the No Exit might come to see that his criminal experience has likely rendered him smarter and more understanding—and then go on to use these qualities to make the system work for him, just as so many other ex-offenders have already done.

It's easier for No Exit corporate inmates. They merely need to believe in their ability to navigate change, and casual investigation will reveal that countless millions of people go on to lead happy lives after overcoming precisely the kinds of travails that No Exit claims to be insurmountable.

8. RAGING ROYALTY

If you want to join in a game of Raging Royalty, then simply stamp your foot and shriek the crucial imprisoning belief: "I'm entitled!"

This extension of the Poison Ivy Syndrome—which we considered earlier—is a favorite among criminal recidivists. "I'm entitled to get high and get laid just as soon as I get out," they wail. "I'm entitled to recover everything the system has stolen from me; to get as much as I can as quickly as I can; to take whatever I want or need to ameliorate my victim status; to be looked after and have someone find me a job; to say whatever I want, when I want; to get angry when the world doesn't treat me right or give me what I want or need; to get high and just forget everything."

The iffy alibi is immediately apparent: "Appearances to the contrary, I'm utterly special—and in jail because the world owes me."* Wounded self-esteem turns to anger and obliterates the capacity of Raging Royalty players even to contemplate how they might achieve virtually anything by dint of personal effort. The grappling style alternates between childlike charm and angry ambivalence—the typical passive-aggressive, in fact.

The liberating counter-belief is this: "Nobody owes me anything and I can satisfy my own realistic needs by virtue of my own efforts, just like any other adult."

---

*"Forty acres and a mule" is sometimes claimed. The derivation of the promise of such a reparation to ex-slaves is unclear, but may have originated from either the First Freedmen's Bureau Act, or efforts of the War Department to provide for the freedmen who marched across Georgia with General Sherman in late 1864 to early 1865. In any event, the covenant is still awaiting fulfillment.

9. SENSITIVE FUGITIVE

Among the homeless roaming the streets and inhabiting the city shelters are many parole violators playing the tragic game of Sensitive Fugitive. The imprisoning belief is this: "I am too vulnerable to survive another jail term." The corollary follows: "Therefore, I won't appear in court and won't go home because the police will come looking for me. I'll exist in the streets instead."

The iffy alibi is spoken softly, if at all: "That's why I can't get my life straightened out." The emotional prism, typically brewed from bitter dregs of an exceptionally unhappy childhood, is fear of just about everyone and everything.

The grappling style is flight. Sensitive Fugitives should really be playing their tragic game within suitably hospitable institutions. In the absence of proper care, however, the liberating counter-beliefs are these: "Running away merely makes things worse. I can handle anything that life throws at me. Jail is just another hotel."

Sensitive Fugitive is also played by corporate inmates. Here, however, the imprisoning belief is slightly different: "I am too vulnerable to survive in the job market." The corollary follows: "Therefore, I'll do absolutely anything to hang on to my current job." When the axe ultimately falls, corporate players typically seek exactly the same role within competitor organizations. What they should be doing, instead of trying to return to the corporate womb, is scouting for something entirely new to fit their deepest underlying talents and desires. But if they could do that, they'd be out of the game.

10. TRAP-OFF

Trap-Off, also common among the homeless, stems from the core imprisoning belief that "the system is out to get me." Parole and probation are thus perceived as mere ruses designed to entrap and to enmesh those reentering society. Trap-Off players may also regard the subway system with extreme suspicion, viewing it as one more aspect of a cunningly devised plan to recapture, resentence, and reincarcerate them. The corollary is clear: "The best way to beat the system is to stay outside it."

Given all of the above, the iffy alibi sounds reasonable: "That's why I reject apparently reasonable offers of help at every turn." The emotional prism, needless to say, is distrust and suspicion following an abusive childhood. The grappling style naturally follows suit: distrustful loner and outsider.

In business, many maverick entrepreneurs view corporations as traps. Their injured self-esteem renders them incapable of ascending within an organizational framework. They're frightened of having to accommodate themselves to the demands and disciplines of corporate life. Many of the small businessmen who speak disparagingly of "big business" are merely playing Trap-Off.

The liberating counter-beliefs are these: "The system is neutral but inconsistent; sometimes it works and sometimes it doesn't. Having the right attitude is a vital part of making it function, however, and I can make it work for me."

The Ultimate Game

"Let me ask you a question, then," I said to Nurturio. "What really might be the best of all games?"

He drew a deep breath, leaned back in his chair and smiled. "It is best," he said, "to believe in yourself and to play the game of Now."

"How do I do that?"

"By knowing your gifts, working at what you love, contributing to others, and living in the moment."

"That's all? There are no other special moves."

"In fact, there are two critical maneuvers. The first is called *carpe diem*, or seize the day. And, once enjoined in the game of Now, the second crucial maneuver is called "follow your heart.""

"No matter where?"

"Correct."

I felt obliged to ask a follow-up question. "I'm sure this is great advice," I said. "But I need to know exactly why playing the game of Now is absolutely the best of all pursuits?"

Nurturio did that deep-breath thing again. "You surely don't need some messiah to come back from the dead," he said, "to remind you that yesterday is only a dream and tomorrow merely a vision." He paused and smiled. "Or that today well lived makes every yesterday a dream of happiness, and every tomorrow a vision of hope."

CHAPTER 18

How to Overcome Temptation

Before It Overcomes You

There are several good protections against temptation
but the surest is cowardice.
—Mark Twain

Evan Colon peers down from his office window to the subway exit below but is lost in thought and sees nothing. He gave notice of his resignation yesterday. It was all very amicable. They asked him to stay on till the end of the month. They might have felt differently if he'd told them he's about to set up in competition. He paces nervously. But will the business come in for him? Compared to his lustrous employer he'll be just a Colon-cum-lately with modest resources. Maybe he'll fall flat on his face. So maybe he should steal—strike that—maybe he should borrow his employer's confidential client list and craft a letter to those fat cats. Hey, all's fair in love and war, right? The boss is out of town so he could maybe even slip his missive into the mail before he finishes up. That really might jump-start things.

Rafael exits the subway onto the pavement and gazes up to the skyscrapers. A shaft of sunlight bathes his face as he sucks the clean spring air. After eight months on Rikers he's back on the streets. He was canned, this time, for stealing. But let's be truthful, his real problem was drugs. He's wearing his entire wardrobe: jeans, tee-shirt, windbreaker, and sneakers. He's got just twenty bucks in his pocket. The immediate problem is to stay clean. If you don't pick it up, you can't use it, right? It sounded so easy when his counselor said it. But nothing's simple on the streets. He studies the avenue. He can turn left and go to that longshot job interview. Or he can turn right and . . .

233

Temptation: "An irresistible force at work on a movable body," said pundit H. L. Mencken. "A thing that attracts, esp. sinful," says the dictionary. A power that impels us to stray from the primrose path to commit an act we know we shouldn't, say I.

We generally can't go about confiding to all and sundry the temptations we managed to resist, so people judge us exclusively by those to which we yield. By my reckoning, the temptation to which we are most likely to succumb inevitably appeals to an innate weakness. For Juan it is drugs to anesthetize himself in the face of the apparently hopeless task of supporting himself within an alien culture. Evan Colon would ordinarily regard Juan's weakness with condescension. Like many he's pitiless toward those whose temptations are not his own. But Evan's inner weakness is remarkably similar. He's contemplating a course of action that could ruin his reputation, because the notion of supporting himself without a corporate umbrella is provoking too much anxiety. If he didn't hanker for self-employment, he might not have a problem. But the idea of becoming "his own man" has proved too tempting. So the combination of ambition and weakness might just turn out to be a deadly force. Shakespeare has Hamlet remark upon the syndrome:

> *So oft it chances in particular men*
> *That for some vicious mole of nature in them . . .*
> *Or by some habit that too much o'erleavens*
> *The form of plausive manners, that these men*
> *Carrying, I say, the stamp of one defect,*
> *Their virtues else—be they as pure as grace,*
> *As infinite as man may undergo—*
> *Shall in the general censure take corruption*
> *From that particular fault.*

Oscar Wilde said he could resist everything except temptation. In fact, temptation sent him to jail. Charging him with committing homosexual acts, a dour prosecutor inquired of Wilde's relationship with a servant boy: "Did you ever kiss him?" Wilde couldn't resist the enticement to flash his famous wit with a facetious put-down: "Oh dear, no—he was a peculiarly plain boy." The prosecutor deftly took the reply as an admission that Wilde had indeed engaged in homosexual relationships, but only with handsome young men. It was all downhill for Wilde from there.

Not everybody wants to overcome temptation. Some make a show of resisting it while not discouraging it completely. After all, a second opportunity might not come quickly. All very understandable, right? Serious temptation shunners—for the moment anyway—might find the following half-dozen injunctions satisfying:

Understand the problem. Roman Catholic dogma calls the underlying defect "original sin." The idea is that we are each born with a specific potentiality to do the wrong thing. According to this concept, there's a defect at the center of our psyches. If we fail to address it, we suffer a predictably unhappy life. Freud noted a related syndrome, repetition-compulsion, the irresistible drive to go on making the same mistake over and over again—the lifelong Sisyphusian quest to roll a stone up the side of a mountain only to have it roll back down again.

Know your poison. One way to identify one's innate defect might be to contemplate the seven deadly sins: pride, wrath, envy, lust, gluttony, avarice, and sloth. We can usually agree on which of our friends and colleagues is susceptible to which sin. Spotting one's own foremost foible, however, is trickier. Fifty-one-year-old Frederick shared his life philosophy in my Rikers class: "It ain't a crime if you don't get caught." I studied him for a moment. "But you *did* get caught, Frederick." I paused. "Can you see any link between your attitude and the fact that two-thirds of your life are gone and you're in jail—again—right now?" Most people imagine that things go wrong in their lives on a random basis. They fail to connect the dots in their problems. They fail to identify the inner defect. They rationalize their untoward behaviors all the way from here to kingdom come.

Don't fool yourself. Mere recognition of one's foible doesn't guarantee immunity from temptation. Sometimes the opposite. Mere contemplation of the sin that brought past pleasure can be enough to spark the lusty desire to commit it again. Lust, says Shakespeare, in sonnet number 129:

. . . is perjured, murderous, bloody, full of blame,
Savage, extreme, rude, cruel, not to trust . . .

Consider John, a brilliant student in his forties. He seemed to have a
handle on his problems yet after a year in jail he "decided" to treat
himself to one last ultimately delicious high on the outside—"for the
good times" as Elvis used to warble. After that, he'd start his new life.
Alas, John got hooked anew, messed up his life, and hated himself for
it. That's temptation for you:

Mad in pursuit, and in possession so . . .
Enjoyed no sooner but despised straight . . .
A bliss in proof, and prov'd, a very woe . . .

Stay out of harm's way. The Chicago Hilton urges guests not to leave
their valuables lying around with a prominent sign proclaiming the
Eleventh Commandment, *Thou Shalt Not Tempt.* Auditors similarly
set up accounting systems on the assumption that people need to be
protected from their underlying weaknesses. Billy Graham confided
that as a young man he never traveled alone with a woman, or ever
permitted himself to be alone in a room with one. I guess he knew
enough about temptation—and his own lusty self—to stay out of
harm's way. The savvy ex-cons who manage to break free of their
problems do so by shunning the "people, places, and things" related
to prior transgressions.

Contemplate the consequences. Juan went to his interview. He didn't get
the job but it led him to something better. He's still struggling, but
proud to call himself a free man and a tax-paying citizen. Evan Colon
purloined that confidential client list. He also mailed his solicitation
for new business prior to the date of his departure. His employer sued.
Evan lost more than the case and damages. These days his name is a
breath of stale air that precedes and follows him wherever he goes. Not
good for the old self-esteem, either.

Delay the impulse. Spiritual advisors tell us not to harbor impure
thoughts. Repent and commit to the right thing now and forever, they

say. This is great advice, but, alas, commitment to a lifetime of purity can seem altogether too daunting. It was Saint Augustine, after all, who prayed, "Lord make me pure, but not yet." More effective for many is to work according to the pragmatic dictum that an impulse is not an act, then beat the mind's demons at their own tricks—telling them lies, offering to sate them somewhere, sometime—but doing the decent thing for yet another day. According to the last lines of that sonnet 129 it's all very clear, but all very difficult, too:

> *All this the world well knows; yet none knows well*
> *To shun the heaven that leads men to this hell.*

CHAPTER 19

Nurturio's Message

In a Nutshell

A man is not determined by what he does
and still less by what he says.
But in the deepest part of himself a being is determined
solely by what he is.
—Charles Péguy

Nurturio's support and counsel have the power to transmute the iron ball of an injured sense of self-esteem into the magic circle of an Intact Sense of Self-Esteem. A process is involved, so the transformation almost certainly won't happen overnight. But as long as we make the necessary effort to incorporate Nurturio's heartfelt counsel into our actual behavior, then magic really can happen.

The Intact Sense of Self-Esteem looks something like this—

Intact Sense of
Self-Esteem

And if we toss that circle and toss it into the air as a conjurer might, like so—

CONFIDENCE

Intact
Sense of
Self-Esteem

then bring it back down and split it into three, like so—

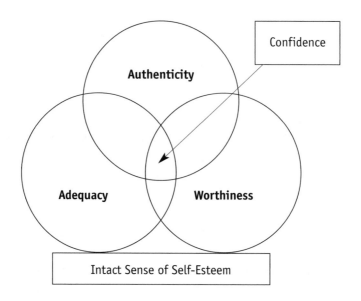

In this set of circles, inner knowledge of Adequacy, Worthiness, and Authenticity create an inner overlap. We'll label the Intact Sense of Self-Esteem, and call the overlap Confidence.

In the end, all the circles come together as the diagram on the next page.

And, now that you're clear on everything, let's see what happens when it all comes together.

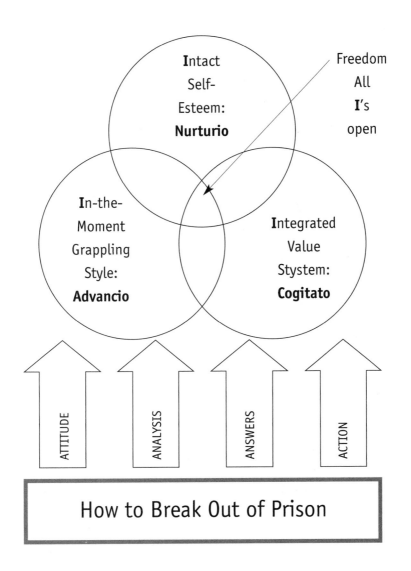

Intact
Self-
Esteem:
Nurturio

Freedom
All
I's
open

In-the-
Moment
Grappling
Style:
Advancio

Integrated
Value
Stystem:
Cogitato

ATTITUDE

ANALYSIS

ANSWERS

ACTION

How to Break Out of Prison

CHAPTER 20

How to Complete a Journey
And Know Where You Are

The longest journey is the journey inwards.

—Dag Hammarskjold

It's a crisp, bright, autumn day and the usually frenetic ride out to Rikers runs surprisingly smoothly. We sign in at the gate and watch the jets roaring in and out of LaGuardia Airport as we drive across the bridge. We park the car, sign in at the second gate, then jam into the rickety, lurching bus that delivers us to cell block C76. We collect our ID tags, pass another security checkpoint, stride down gleaming, disinfected corridors through yet another two sets of sliding iron gates, then descend down three flights of stairs to the classroom.

The waiting class of thirty souls sizes up my guest. His immaculate dark suit, crisp white shirt, and neatly knotted, understated tie are giveaways. He's a corrections department big shot, surely.

I pause for silence. "Good morning! And please welcome our guest, Mr. Rafael Phoenix." The applause is polite but sincere. Spirits inevitably rise when somebody important seems to be paying attention. "Rafael has taken the morning off from his regular job to be with us here today. I could say a lot about him, but I know he'll do a better job of introducing himself than I ever could."

I step to a seat in the back of the room. Rafael glances over the up-turned faces, takes a deep breath, and waits for total silence. . . .

"I know you but you don't know me, so let me make a confession. I served nine years in upstate New York prisons. I wasn't a model inmate, and when I got out I wasn't a model citizen, either. I smoked crack and added three new arrests and convictions to my fifteen-page rap sheet. I got rearrested after only four measly months. Suddenly, at age thirty-six I was back in prison and sitting in the chairs that you're sitting in right now. So like I said, I know you. I know how you think and I know why you're here. Your mere presence in this room tells me a whole lot about you." He pauses. "It also tells me a whole lot about the person I used to be."

He's won them over instantly. Confidence can do that. His natural intensity—his gravitas, actually—is helping, too.

"My life changed in this very classroom when somebody asked me the question, 'What quality of life do you really want for yourself?' The idea that I even had a life to take charge of had never really occurred to me. I'd effectively been dead from the neck up for years. But that question began an awakening. Suddenly, I couldn't get that quality-of-life idea out of my mind. Then a teacher told me that I was a lost soul but a decent and talented person. That last bit of that sentence came as a new idea, too. But I took it all to heart, just the same."

In fact, Rafael was an ideal student. He read every handout and participated in exercises. Something certainly touched him. Maybe that something was everything.

"Six months later I quit this place with three subway tokens in my pocket and a burning desire in my heart. On the train back into the city I dreamed of an infinitely better life. Today, barely twelve months later, I'm living that dream. I'm buying the things I used to steal. I work hard and earn good money in an office down by the South Street Seaport. I've bought some nice clothes. I eat in the local restaurants and the waiters call me sir. I talk to my friends on my cell phone. I even have a bank account. In the past I was always one argument away from being homeless. Today I'm about to sign a lease on my own apartment. Who'd have believed it? Hey, quality of life—it's out there. We've each got to find it for ourselves, of course, but I've got three suggestions that might help."

A teacher hopes to say something—nobody knows exactly what—that might just release the genie from the bottle. Sometimes it happens and sometimes it doesn't. But the genie's the genie—all the teacher ever did was rub the bottle.

"First, give yourself a chance. When I got out on parole I was thirty-seven years old. I'd never had my own apartment or paid my own bills. What kind of example was that for my fifteen-year-old son? In the past, I returned to the home of either my mother or some chick. But that never worked out. Not for anyone. I'd get up in the morning and say I was going off to find work. Then I'd spend the day hustling trouble with the old gang. We always found it, too. So this time around I signed on for a room in a halfway house. Just about none of you guys are going to even try to do that. You're thinking, I'm gonna get out of jail and smoke me a fat one, drink me a Heineken, then go out and lay Shorty. In the past I'd have joined you. Not today, however, because I know how that movie ends. You find a man to offer you a blunt and you say, 'Ah, let's just take a couple drags'—and, suddenly, you're off to the races. But, listen to me, now—as long as you go off lollygagging and dragging your feet, the doors you need to pass through will either stay closed or they'll get shut in your face."

He's talking their language and he's right. A new attitude has to precede all else. But when that transformation happens, miracles can follow.

"So, second, create some lucky breaks. Opportunities just don't come. You've got to hustle for them. So get on the phone, find some leads, run them to ground, and keep on keeping on. Lucky breaks generally come disguised as hard work and some people can't see past appearances. They say, I'm not gonna take no rotten messenger job. But that's a job that takes you to just about every employer in the city. A messenger can drop his resume a dozen times a day. Another way to create luck is to present yourself like a serious person. My hair used to be long—almost as long as a couple of the Afros I'm looking at right now. But when I got out last time, I decided I needed to make another kind of impression. I didn't want to be held back by appearances. I said to myself, Rafael, you've got nothing in your pocket except lint and an ID card, so don't let a wild mane of hair get between you and a job. So I shaved that Afro right off. When I've made it big, I'll wear my hair any way I want. Meantime I'm working on the principle that when you act the part you want, you get the thing you want. That's why I'm always looking and acting like a candidate for serious promotion."

Rafael has clenched his fist to emphasize the point. He knows that this a tough message for some of these guys to hear. He knows that they cling to their old identities out of both pride and fear.

"Third, make a clean break with the past. When I got out of jail the last time, I went and got my gun. Then I rode to the river and flung it into the deepest water. If I'd merely hung it up somewhere, I'd have been able to pick it up whenever life didn't seem to be going my way. But now I can't be tempted. That's important because I don't have the luxury of relapsing. If I smoke crack, I'm smoking everything. I'll be running for the rest of my life. I know people who'll give me drugs. But I've scrapped those so-called friends, too. Letting go of your old life isn't easy. And, when you're getting out of jail achieving independence can seem impossible. But remember this: you're merely scrapping the crutches that crippled you, and ridding yourself of a bunch of enablers who condoned all the wrong things." He pauses. "And when you shed that baggage life'll change, once and for all." He cracks a smile. "Somebody might even ask you to come back here and give a little talk. Hey, thanks for listening. You got the message, right?"

Applause and a chorus of whoops answer that question.

One of the most spectacular views of the Manhattan skyline is also the most melancholy. I'm talking about the view from the bridge as you're departing Rikers Island. The Twin Towers are gone, of course. Yet it's almost impossible not to rebuild them in the mind's eye. I drive slowly, and we take it all in.

"Looks like the Land of Oz," says Rafael.

"Yeah—and in a way I guess it is." I pause. "So how did all that feel?"

"It was giving me an ache and it gave me a high."

"How so?"

"It was unsettling to see my old attitudes reflected in those guys. It was like I was talking to myself—to the punk I used to be."

"And . . ."

"And I got a kick because they seemed to listen."

"They certainly did."

"So"—he pauses—"do you think I might've made a difference?"

How should I answer that? Shall I say that he touched their lives as absolutely nobody else ever could? Shall I say that his words turned minds and his authenticity transformed hearts? Shall I say that he altered the colors and climate of my own emotional universe? I'm mulling these questions when the answer appears. "I sure as hell hope so," I hear myself say.

Rafael shoots me a serious glance. I return it, deadpan.

Then we break into laughter.

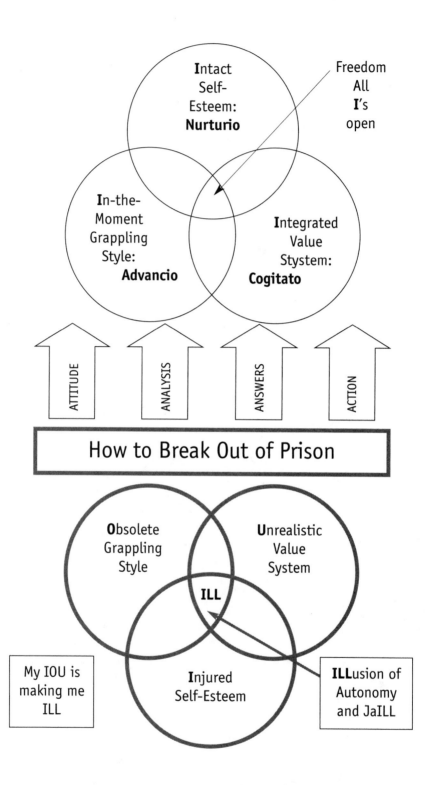

John Wareham, founder and principal of Wareham Associates, leadership psychologists, is author of several best-selling books on the human side of management, including the bestselling *Secrets of a Corporate Headhunter,* and the 13-language reference classic, *Anatomy of a Great Executive,* as well as a critically acclaimed novel that explores moral quandaries. An award-winning speaker—former national oratory champion, and "hands down winner" among business communicators according to the *Financial Times*—John has led and keynoted symposiums for corporate leaders throughout the world. In addition to his corporate work he is President of The Eagles Foundation of America, Inc., whose mission is to identify and develop leaders from within the prison population.

On the web:
corporate: *www.wareham.org*
pro bono: *www.eaglesusa.org*
Authors Guild site:
www. johnwareham.com

Wareham is a boutique consultancy whose mission is to provide sophisticated solutions to leadership problems, thereby helping sophisticated organizations optimize investment in intellectual capital.

◆ We help CEOs to appoint executive winners, gain precise insight into senior management strengths and weaknesses, and build synergistic executive teams.

◆ We help individual team members realize their personal potential: developing leadership talent and enabling achievers to build on strength.

These goals are addressed with unique, proprietary instruments and methodologies:

◆ The *Elevation Evaluation*, providing deep, confidential, whole-person insight into the makeup and motivations of senior executives being considered for higher appointment.

◆ The *Leadership Style Doctor*, providing executives with unique insight into development needs and practical, focused personal development prescriptions.

◆ *Transceptual Adjustment*. Customized one-on-one counseling to unleash the full potential of senior and fast-track executives.

◆ *Team Building Treatments*. Retreats where John Wareham leads uniquely powerful, galvanizing development seminars in the vital areas of:

  ◆   advanced leadership selection
  ◆   communication and presentation
  ◆   advanced leadership development.

www.wareham.org

Wareham Wit & Wisdom
in a Stunning New Novel

LEADERSHIP, LOVE, AND ENLIGHTENMENT
Nothing was quite as it seemed . . .

On the day his big-time dreams seem about to come true, Chandler Haste glances into the rearview mirror of the limousine bearing him across Manhattan's Triboro bridge, and catches the reflection of a scorching affair from his past over-leaping oceans to engulf him.

Welcome Rain Publishers